THE NATIONALISTIC AND RELIGIOUS LECTURES OF SWAMI VIVEKANANDA

CONDENSED & RETOLD BY
SWAMI TAPASYANANDA

Advaita Ashrama
(Publication Department)
5 Dehi Entally Road
Calcutta 700 014

Published by
Swami Mumukshananda
President, Advaita Ashrama
Mayavati, Champawat, Himalayas
from its Publication Department, Calcutta

© *All Rights Reserved*
First Edition, January 1990
First Reprint, June 1998
3M3C

ISBN 81-7505-090-X

Printed in India at
Gipidi Box Co.
3B Chatu Babu Lane
Calcutta 700 014

PUBLISHER'S NOTE TO THE SECOND EDITION

Swami Vivekananda was a manifold personality — a spiritual gaint, who, not satisfied with his own unfoldment, intensely strove for the good of all. Whatever he did or spoke, it was for the salvation of India, for the removal of the misery of the world, and above all, how every human being could get the knowledge of his divinity. Swamiji's message was, therefore, not for one time, but for all times; not for one country, but for all countries.

In India, a large number of people are drawn to Swamiji because of his great love for his country. He is called a 'patriot saint'. To them he was more an awakener of India than an awakener of souls. But to the devotees and followers of Swamiji the world over, the story is different. They admire and turn to him because his spiritual message of strength, hope and courage opens up new vistas to them.

The present book is a summarized version of some of the lectures and writings of Swamiji. We hope its thorough reading will gradually lead the reader to go to the original lectures and enable him to derive the full benefit of Swamiji's blessing and inspiration.

The first edition of this book was published by Sri Ramakrishna Math, Madras. Since the copyright has been made over to us, we deem it a privilege to offer this book to the public.

PUBLISHER

18 January 1990
Advaita Ashrama
Mayavati, Himalayas

PREFACE

This book entitled the '*Nationalistic and Religious Lectures of Swami Vivekananda*' is the last of the series of three books planned for giving in a short compass a summarised version of the main contents of the Works of Swami Vivekananda published in eight volumes. The sections of his Works which comprise his letters, interviews, poems etc. could not be included in this scheme of abridgement.

Unlike in the previous volumes, the contents of this do not deal entirely with lectures. Several of the items like Modern India, The East and the West, Memoirs of European Travels etc., are not lectures but writings translated from Bengali into English, and they deal not mainly with religion but with the historical development of the cultural life of the world.

The most important part of the Volume is wherein the replies of the Swami to the addresses presented to him on his return to India are summarised. These great orations of the Swami should form a subject of serious study for all Indians to recapture the spiritual values that we are fast forgetting on account of the rising tide of secularism patronised by many modern Indian leaders. The Swami points out in these lectures what the genuine brand of Indian nationalism should be.

Sri Ramakrishna Math,
Madras.   PUBLISHERS.
19-5-1985

INTRODUCTION
Swami Vivekananda's Theory of Indian Nationalism

The lectures and writings of Swami Vivekananda, summarised and retold in this book, though devoted mainly to the religion and culture of India, have also a direct bearing on Indian nationalism. They develop a particular theory of nationalism which is in the main opposed to the current ideas of it. These expositions of the ideals of Indian nationalism occur in the replies he gave to the addresses of welcome that were presented to him on his return to India, when he travelled from Colombo to Calcutta and from there to the Punjab and Kashmir. They are published in the book called *'Lectures from Colombo to Almora'*. These lectures of the Swami comprise only half a volume out of the eight such volumes of his published Works. They are unique in respect of the fact that they are the only lectures he delivered on Indian soil, while all the rest, dealing with various aspects of Vedanta, were given from the world platforms of America and England. Therefore, it is in these lectures that we come across Swamiji's patriotic fervour and the way in which his spiritual ideology shaped his patriotic zeal. They reveal Swami Vivekananda the patriot-saint.

The Swami's return to India after his successful mission to the West and the tremendous enthusiasm it generated at the time were unique events even in the long history of India. For a thousand years India had been subjected to foreign invasions and foreign rule. The last and the most significant of these was the British occupation of India. A company of merchants coming from far across the seas and defeating with their comparatively small forces, the big armies of powers that were considered mighty and invincible for centuries, and organising a government that was efficient and law-enforcing, had a stunning effect on the classes and the masses of India. Above all, familiarity with the culture and the language of these new conquerors brought the intellectuals of the country face to face with a system of thought and ways of organisation which impressed them as far superior to anything they had indigenously. While this shock treatment might have done some good in awakening them from their complacency and conceit born of the systematic isolationism they had been practising for long, its evil effects began to manifest when it took the shape of a cultural submission and an abject imitative spirit as also a total condemnation of India's past. All the signs of a cultural decadence, leading to cultural death, began to come to the surface.

Another effect, one much more healthy, of the British occupation of India was the help it gave to the consolidation of the incipient sense of nationalism prevailing in the country. India, a geographical expression bounded by the Himalayas in the North and the seas on the three sides, had always the sense of a cultural unity, but it could not in the past develop into what is today called the sentiment of nationalism, for two reasons. The multiplicity of States and the want of a linguistic link for its sprawling parts, save for the prevalence of Sanskrit as a sacred language, stood in the way of the development of a strong sense of nationhood. The establishment of the British Government remedied both these deficiencies. Practically the whole of India came under a common central government with a common administrative set up. The English language, though known only to the educated elite, became a common link language used for administration, education, legal system etc., all over the country. It served also as a window for communication with the world at large.

Swami Vivekananda's appearance on the world scenario was the first sign of the awakening of India from the stupor into which it had fallen before and after the British conquest, into a consciousness of its identity as a nation and its importance in the comity of nations. Swamiji's tremendous success in the West as an exponent of the spiritual message of India was a surprising shock to the detractors of Indian culture and a stimulating leaven to its enthusiastic protagonists. India, it was felt, was not certainly face to face with its cultural doom when a pure and authentic exponent of it could draw so much of acclamation at the hands of the races that dominated the world at the time. It resulted in the resuscitation of the national sense of self-respect.

Besides, in Swami Vivekananda the whole country saw a common leader—their man, irrespective of the language or region, who represented their ideals and aspirations. So the whole country joined in giving him a reception of a magnitude that India had never witnessed before. The welcome took almost the shape of a mass movement. The whole of his journey from Colombo to Almora had the appearance of a triumphal march representing a national revival, and not merely that of functions organised for honouring a religious personality. After the establishment of the British power in India, this was the first stirring of the spirit of nationalism in India, which was finally to lead through successive stages to Indian Independence in 1947.

In the course of his journey from Colombo northwards, he was presented with addresses of welcome in various cities of India, and to these he gave stirring replies. In these, as also in the independent lectures he gave, all of which are now embodied in the volume 'Lectures From Colombo to Almora', he has given to the Indian people a perennial source of patriotic inspiration, scintillating with the great spiritual ideals of the nation.

In these lectures he exhorted Indians not to condemn their social and cultural past and take to a life of imitation of the West. That is the way to sure and certain doom. Nor should they merely exalt the past and refuse to move forward. That is the way to stagnation and decadence. India has a glorious heritage. In religion and philosophy it has been the teacher of the world all through the ages. It retains its genius in this respect even today. Revival of spirituality has always been the prelude to the revival of cultural and political life in India. For, spirituality is the soul of India. Its enhancement has always been the sure way to greatness, and its erosion, the way to national suicide.

From his study of world history, he expounded a theory regarding the survival of nations, and he applied it to explain the cause of India's survival in spite of all the disasters that threatened to destroy it. He maintained that human history shows that every nation has to make a contribution of its own in a chosen field for the general advancement of humanity and that when it ceases to do so it decays and dies. Nature effaces it off to make way for more vigorous and younger races to take up the role. For, it is Nature's practice to get rid of an atrophied part of an organism and let others take up its function. Thus there have been great nations in the past, the Egyptians, the Babylonians, the Persians, the Greeks, the Romans etc., whose civilisations were parallel in time with that of India. But they have all disappeared from the face of the earth and the regions where they flourished are now occupied by people whose culture and national histories have no continuity with those of these ancient people. The reason for it, according to Swami Vivekananda, is the fact that they ceased to fulfil their national purpose, which were mostly political, social, military etc. After short periods of vigorous national life, they lost their hold on the national theme which made them great, and this led to their gradual decay and ultimate destruction at the hands of more vigorous people.

India also has been having a national theme through the whole of its history, the beginnings of which are beyond the capacity of man to reckon. That theme of India's specialisation is spirituality, which means the adoption of ways of life that lead to an immediate perception of the truth of the Atman and of God, even in this embodied state. All through her history, in spite of invasion and foreign subjugation, India has been producing men with this spiritual insight; and from this country have gone forth waves of movements that have brought spiritual light and wisdom to the nations of the world.

Even today, India retains this capacity. It was during the early days of British occupation, when India was threatened with cultural effacement at the hands of the victorious West, that the greatest of our spiritual men was born in the person of Sri Ramakrishna. Thus, in spite of political subjection and economic impoverishment, India has all through the ages been keeping itself alive as a nation, as is evident from the abundance of its vitality in this, its chosen field of specialisation. The moment India abandons its spiritual ideal—the acceptance of realisation of the spiritual essence in man and

the world as the goal of human life—,its national life will be
threatened with imminent extinction.

This insistence on the spiritual ideal does not mean that
in Swamiji's scheme of national reconstruction there is no
place for the eradication of poverty and improvement of man's
material life. He was of the view that it is no good preaching
spiritual doctrines to hungry stomachs. Man has to be
above the poverty line and should be in good physical health
if he is to undergo spiritual disciplines. India no doubt
adored poverty, but it was not the wretchedness of want
but the non-covetuous and non-possessive attitude of mind of
the sage, rich in the wealth of the Spirit. The spiritual
upliftment of man therefore includes the upliftment of the
material conditions of his life. So in the Indian lectures
summarised in this volume we find powerful exhortations by
the Swami for the improvement of the living conditions of
people in India, but at the same time warnings too against
making material comfort and a high standard of living the be-
all and end-all of life, as has been done in the West. Dharma
(morality), Artha (wealth and power), Kama (pleasure), and
Moksha (liberation)—have all been recognised by Indian
scriptures as values relevant to human life. But the pursuit
of them must be regulated in a way that the fulfilments
they offer ultimately lead to Moksha. Spiritual values are
the ultimate. Material values are desirable to the extent
they subserve and help the development of the former, but
are never ends in themselves.

In these lectures summarised herein, SwamiVivekananda
warns Indians to ply their national ship very carefully between
the two sources of danger, the Scylla of Western materialism
and the Charybdis of Eastern obscurantism. Spirituality

is cultivation of the great ideals taught in the Gita and the Upanishads in such a way that they are reflected in our individual and national life. The practice of village customs, caste rules, don't-touchism, irrational usages in eating and drinking—these have nothing to do with spirituality. Social rules and practices have changed from time to time. They do not represent the eternal values. Too much insistence on these externals to the detriment of the real and eternal spiritual principles expounded in the Gita and the Upanishads, have been the main baneful influence that has been vitiating the life of the people. When Swamiji exhorts us to retain our hold on our spiritual ideals, he is not asking us to relapse into this nightmare of social and religious obscurantism, but to be forward-looking and to go ahead without forgetting the great teachings of the Gita and the Upanishads. We have to learn plenty from the West in the fields of organisation, science, politics and technology for the improvement of our social and economic conditions. Our deficiency in these respects is largely the result of the mania for exclusiveness and avoidance of contact with the external world that crept into the soul of the nation at some times past in its history. When the world marched forward in science and technology, India remained smug in its own shell, glorifying itself in its don't-touchism, caste obsession and kitchen religion. This kind of orthodoxy should go, and the progressive spirit of the West captured, without losing our moorings in the Upanishads and the Gita. Progressiveness must be informed and directed by sensitiveness to spiritual values.

It is worthwhile considering whether the India of today has been following the ideal of nationalism preached by Swami Vivekananda. No doubt the political leaders at the helm of affairs have been doing their best, though not in a

way that is very satisfactory, to ameliorate poverty and illi-
teracy and to improve the living conditions of the people.
But the State maintains that secularism is the main principle
of all its policies.   Secularism in political science means only
that the State does not identify itself with any religion, that
all religions are alike for the State, that religious institutional
heads and ideologies have got nothing to do with the government of a country, and that a religious nomenclature does
not entitle any one to any special right.   But should a secular
State be irreligious or anti-religious, as it is in purely com-
munistic States?   In India, as matters stand today, the State
does not go to the extent of persecuting religion.   It is satisfied
to remain neutral.   But the effect of this so-called religious
neutrality has been the development of the attitude of indiffe-
rence to religion and as a consequence, to spiritual values too.

A question may be raised here whether there is a necessary
connection between religion and spiritual values. There
is a section of forward-looking people today who decry
religiosity but contend that this does not tantamount to
decrying spirituality, for they maintain that religiosity and
spirituality are different and that a man can be spiritual
without being religious.   While there is a good deal of releva-
nce in this attitude, there is also a great flaw in it, as in
saying that it is the wine that is important and not its container. The blunder here is obvious. For, the wine has
always depended on the container for its preservation.   In
human history, religions have always been the containers of
spiritual values.   For, religion has provided through the ages
the forms and symbols, the concepts and the imageries
through which spiritual values have been preached, observed
and transmitted in all societies. So there is an indissoluble
nexus between religion and spirituality.

While there is nothing inherently wrong in this association, difficulties arise because religions, as practised in most societies, have included in their scope many values other than what are purely spiritual. Religious affiliations have often been one of the principal bases for forming communal-political groups and parties, with the inevitable consequence that religion is politicised and converted into a mainstream for conveying the dirty effluents of human relations. Thus in world history wars have been fought, murder, loot and arson let loose and whole countries ravaged in the name of religion. In India itself, it is a well-known fact that in our recent history the country was divided into two in the name of religion.

As a consequence, religion has got a bad name among a large body of politically minded people, and the elimination of its influence and the replacement of it by what they call 'secularism' is considered by them as a panacea for all the evils that beset our body politic. But has this secularisation produced the desired result? Has it eliminated war? Has it improved the nature of human relations? Has it contributed to the happiness of man in general? From what we know of conditions in our country and outside, secularism has in no way accomplished these expectations. On the other hand, its protagonists have, by breaking the bottle of religion succeeded only in spilling away whatever little spiritual value it contained. In India we find today that in proportion to the rising tide of secularisation, corruption, deception, immorality etc., have increased. The thirty and odd years of secularisation show that spiritual values cannot be conserved and propagated without the help of the religious medium. The defect has not been with religion as such, but with the way in which it has been politicised and misinterpreted by bad men.

To free religion from the social and political abuses that have brought it a bad name, it is to be made to function under certain limitations. Some of these may be stated thus: (1) Religions should become more a matter of realisation than of dogmatism. (2) Fundamentalism in religion should be discouraged, and every man must be free to interpret and follow his religion without any external or organisational compulsions. (3) Religion should not be allowed to obstruct the evolution of a common civil law. (4) No kind of social institution that goes against human dignity should be allowed to exist and justify itself in the name of religion. (5) Religious conversions must be barred by law, as these conversions are effected mainly from political motives, and will ultimately go against national integration. This does not deny the freedom for spiritual conversion, which does not require a change of one's original social and cultural affiliation—not even of one's religious nomenclature. Reconversion of people who were converted by force or by being misguided should, however, be allowed. (6) Religious freedom should mean only the right to practise a religion and preach it among its own adherents and admirers for their improvement, and not to take an aggressive stance against other religionists, or to criticise and caricature their beliefs and practices. (7) The study of comparative religion should become an important subject in the curricula of studies adopted in schools and colleges. In a multi-religious country like India, the text books suitable for students of different standards must be prepared, not by fundamentalists of different reli-gions, but by enlightened people who accept the validity of all religions. These text books must give the principal teachings of all religions in a way that the students may have respect for all religions, and not a contemptuous or hostile attitude. Only then can the followers of different religions be exposed to the teachings of all religions.

In place of harping on secularism, the State has to assume a more active role in generating among the growing generation an awareness of religion in the right perspective suited to a multi-racial and multi-religious society like that of India. Education is today in the hands of the State, and it is open to the State to include in the syllabi the study of religions through selections from scriptures and text books written by non-sectarian writers, with a good knowledge of comparative religion. The followers of differnt religions should be exposed to the best presentation of religions other than theirs. This will enable the growing generations to understand the strength and greatness of all religions, and thus prepare their minds to the acceptance of the validity of all religions and to the exclusion of fanaticism. The preservation of a healthy religious attitude is an absolute necessity, if spiritual values are to be preserved. If men eschew all spiritual values, human society will degenerate into a society of clever animals deliberately indulging in evil activities which even animals do not indulge in.

In the *Lectures from Colombo to Almora* Swami Viveka-nanda has therefore warned the nation that if they throw religion overboard, they will be throwing away spiritual values too, and thereby they will be paving the way for the extinction of India as a nation with a cultural identity. It is high time that the prophets of secularism paid heed to this warning.

CONTENTS

		PAGE
PREFACE	.. ..	iii
INTRODUCTION	.. ..	V-XV

1. **On Hinduism at the Parliament of Religions** ..   1-11

Response to welcome, 1—Why We Disagree, 1—
The Hindu Scriptures, 2—Truth of the Atman and
Reincarnation, 3—Doctrine of Isvara, 5—Sri
Krishna's Doctrine of Love and Non-attachment,
6—Doctrine of Mukti or Liberation, 7—The
Advaitic Development of the above Doctrines,
7—The Truth about Image worship, 8—The Harmony of Religions, 9—Universality of Hinduism,
10—Address at the Final Session, 10.

2. **On Hinduism**   12-17

India as the Punya Bhumi, 12—Religion as the
Prime concern in India, 13—The Need of India's
Spiritual Ideals in the West, 14—Laws, Eternal
and Temporary, 15—The Ideal of Universal
Acceptance, 15.

3. **Vedantism**   18-24

The Scriptures of Hinduism, 18—Essential points
common to all Hindus: Theory of Creation, 19—
Doctrine of God, 20—The Doctrine of the Atman,
21—The Personal and the Impersonal Ideas of
God, 22—The Doctrine of Ishtam, 23.

4. **Address at Pamban**   25

N-ii

N—2

5.   **Real Worship**   26

6.   **India's Great Spiritual Men**   27-29
     Spirituality the foundation of India's national
     life, 27—The Two Dangers ahead, 28.

7.   **Vedanta as the Ideal Religion**   30-31

8.   **The Path of Progress for India**   32-33

9.   **Eternal and Changing Phases of Religion**   ..   34-35

10. **Mission of Vedanta**   36-41
     Spiritual Orientation of Religion in India, 36—
     Vedanta as the true Universal Religion: Prin-
     ciple versus Personality, 37—Harmony of Reli-
     gions in India, 38—Unity of Existence, 39—The
     Way for the uplift of India, 40.

11. **My Plan of Campaign**   42-47
     Some critical remarks, 42—Criticism of
     Reformers and their ways, 43—How the Ancient
     Masters effected changes, 44—The True Ideal of
     Patriotism, 46.

12. **Vedanta and its Application to Indian Life**   ..   48-53
     Vedantism is Hinduism, 48—The Upanishads
     and their all-inclusiveness, 48—The Upanishads
     as a Doctrine of Unity and Strength, 50—The
     Upanishads should be preached to all, 52.

13. **The Work Before us**   54-59
     The Greek and the Indian, 54—Causes of India's
     Downfall, 55—Need for the Expansion of India's
     Spiritual Culture, 56—The Uniqueness and Har-
     mony of Vedic Thought, 57.

14. **The Future of India** 60-64
Why we should think of the Past, 60—Solution of
the caste and ethnic problems, 61—The Way to
build up our Future, 63.

15. **The Sages of India** 65-70
Vedanta gives precedence to Principle over Per-
sonalities, 65—Vedanta recognises the Sages and
Incarnations of all Religions 66—Incarnations;
Rama and Krishna, 67—The Buddha, 68—
Sankara and Ramanuja, 69—Sri Ramakrishna,
the Fulfilment of the Line of Indian Sages, 70.

16. **Reply to the Address at Calcutta** 71-74
About Work in the West, 71—Significance of Sri
Ramakrishna, 72—Spiritual Expansion of India,
73.

17. **The Vedanta in all its Phases** 75-83
Hindu Scriptures and their Characteristics, 75—
Impersonality of the Upanishads, 78—Some
Common points of Agreement among Vedantic
Schools, 78—What is Purity of Food? 79—
Dualists and Non-dualists, a Contrast, 80—Ren-
unciation, the chief Condition for growth of
Spirituality, 81—The Truth about Individuality,
82.

18. **Address of Welcome at Almora** 84

19. **The Common Bases of Hinduism** 85-89
Spirituality as the Heart of India, 85—Agreement
among the various sects of India, 86—Divinity of
the Soul, 87—The Conditions for India's Regeneration, 88.

20. **The Religion We are Born in**   90-92
Veda, the Scripture of Hindus, 90—The Common
Principles of our Religion, 91.

21. **Reply to the Madras Address**   93-97
Realisation as the Test of Religious Truth, 93—
Deathless India, 94—The World Needs Indian
Thought, 95—Divinity of the Spirit in Man, 95.

22. **Causes of India's Downfall and Ways of
Reconstruction**   98-100
Isolation from world community, 98—Pseudo-
renunciation, 99—The abandonment of the
original idea of Jati, 99

23. **My Life and Mission**   101-103
India Decadent, not Dead, 101—Regeneration
through Sannyasa, 102.

24. **Women of India**   104-106
Woman as Mother, 104—Woman as Wife and
Daughter, 104—Widowhood, 105—Daughter in
the Family, 106.

25. **Modern India**   107-119
Pre-Buddhistic Polity in India, 107—Rise of
Kingly Power in the Buddhist Age, 108—Muslim
Rule and Resurgence of Imperialism, 109—East
India Company and Rise of Merchant Power,
110—The Ages of Dominance of the Priest, the
King, the Merchant and the Worker, 111—
Priestly Power, its Achievement and Failings,
112—Kingly power, its Achievement and Fail-
ings, 114—Merchant Power, its Achievements

and Failings, 114—Total Degradation of India to
Sudrahood, 116—Rise of Sudra Power in the
future, 117—Awakening of India, 117.

26. **The East and the West**   120-145
The Misconceived Picture of the Cultures, 120—
The National Ideal, 121—Dharma and Moksha
Ideals, 122—Freedom from the Tyranny of the
Moksha Ideal, 124—The Balanced Outlook of
Vedic Religion, 124—Hinduism, a Living Entity,
125—Who are the Aryans, 127—Progressiveness,
128—Cleanliness and Elegance, 129—On Matters
of Food, 130—Civilisation in Dress and Manners,
134—France and its Capital Paris, 136—Social
Evolution in the East and the West, 138—Rise of
Civilisations of Asia and Europe, 141—Rise of
Islam and the Crusades, 142—Progressive Civili-
sation, the Western and the Eastern, 144

27. **The Great Teachers of the World**   146-150
The necessity for a multiplicity of Prophets and
Incarnations, 146—The Message of Krishna, 148
—The Message of the Buddha, 149—The Message
of Christ, 150—The Message of Mohammed, 150

28. **My Master**   151-165
The Occidental and the Oriental Ideals of Civili-
sed Life, 151—The Cultural Milieu in India in
the Mid-nineteenth Century, 153—Sri Rama-
krishna and his Spiritual quest, 154—Arrival of
Teachers, 157—Marriage and after, 158—Other
Spiritual Practices, 159—As a Teacher, 160—
God can be Experienced, 161—Harmony of
Religions, 161—Renunciation as the Soul of his

Life and Teachings, 163—Love of fellow beings,
163.

29.   Hinduism and Sri Ramakrishna   166-168

30.   Pavhari Baba   169-174

31.   The Buddha's Message   175-180
      Priests and Prophets,   175—Religious Life in
      India when the Buddha appeared, 176—His doc-
      trines, 176—Vedantic View contrasted with the
      Buddhistic Teaching, 178—Legacy of Buddhism,
      179.

32.   On Lord Buddha   181

33.   Buddhism the Fulfilment of Hinduism   182-183

34.   Christ the Messenger   184-189
      The Necessity of a Humanised God, 184—The
      Background of Jesus Christ, 184—Jesus stood for
      Renunciation and Realisation, 185—Three levels
      of Spiritual Teachings, 187—The Spiritual Ideal
      of Jesus is today forgotten, 188.

35.   Notes from Several Discourses and Lectures   ..   190-203
      On Karma Yoga, 190—On Fanaticism, 191—
      Work is worship, 191—Work without Motive,
      192—Sadhanas or Preparations for Higher Life,
      193—The Cosmos and the Self, 195—Who is a
      Real Guru? 196—On Art, 197—On Language,
      197—Isvara and Brahman, 198—On Jnana Yoga,
      198—What is the Cause of Illusion? 200—
      Evolution, 201—Buddhism and Vedanta, 201—
      Law and Freedom, 202.

THE NATIONALISTIC AND RELIGIOUS LECTURES OF SWAMI VIVEKANANDA

ON HINDUISM AT THE PARLIAMENT OF RELIGIONS*

Response to Welcome

It fills my heart with joy unspeakable to rise in response to the warm and cordial welcome given by you. I thank you in the name of the most ancient Order of Monks of the world. I thank you in the name of the mother of religions and millions and millions of the Hindu people of all classes and sects.

I am going to talk about a religion which has taught the world both tolerance and universal acceptance. I am proud to belong to a nation which has sheltered the persecuted and the refugees of all religions and all nations of the world. We believe that just as all the rivers having different sources mingle in the same water of the sea, so all the religions in spite of the differences in their origin and methods lead to the same God. I fervently hope that the bells that tolled this morning in honour of this convention may be the death-knell of all fanaticism and of all persecutions by word or deed.

Why We Disagree

The followers of different religions quarrel and fight among themselves because of the narrowness of their outlook and their failure to understand that the Supreme Being is infinite. The attitude of each religion is like that of the proverbial frog in the well. The story goes that the frog in the well happened to meet a frog from the sea, and it tried to estimate and understand from the latter the size of the sea in

---

*Vol. I, p. 3. Delivered at Chicago.

terms of the distance it could cover by taking leaps in the well. When the sea frog said that it was nonsense to compare the sea with the well, the frog of the well retorted that the former must be a liar, as nothing could be bigger than his well. The trouble with us is very much similar. Each religionist sits in the small well of his religion and thinks that the spiritual truth is exhausted by the conceptions of his religion. They forget that the spiritual truth relates to God, the Infinite Being, who cannot be measured by any of our humanly restricted standards.

The Hindu Scriptures

There are three religions beginning from pre-historic times —Hinduism, Zoroastrianism and Judaism. Of these Judaism has been ousted from its own place of birth by its all-conquering daughter Christianity. As for Zoroastrianism, it has been wiped out of existence but for the handful of Parsis who had taken refuge in India. Hinduism, however, has survived the shock of numerous invasions, and in course of time, has succeeded in absorbing and assimilating most of the cultures that threatened its existence.

The scope of the Hindu faith extends from the high flights of Vedanta philosophy to practices like image worship and the multifarious mythologies of the Puranas. Even the agnosticism of the Buddhists and the atheism of the Jains have a place in it. We have to understand what is that common centre to which all the radii of these varying faiths converge.

The Hindus have received their religion through revelation, the Vedas. The Vedas are eternal, without beginning or end. By the Vedas no books are meant but eternal spiritual laws discovered by different sages of different times like scientific laws. These discoverers of the spiritual realm are called the Rishis, whom we consider as perfect beings.

But it may be asked that while laws may not have an end, they must have had a beginning from the start of creation. The Vedas declare, however, that creation is without a beginning and an end, but is an eternally going process in cycles of manifestations and dissolutions. Creation and the creator are like two parallel lines without a beginning and an end. 'God (the Creator) is the ever active Providence, by whose power systems after systems are being evolved out of chaos, made to run for a time and again destroyed, to come out again in the next cycle of creation.' So runs the commonly repeated Mantra,'The sun and the moon, the Lord created like the suns and the moons of the previous cycles.'

Truth of the Atman and Reincarnation

When one closes one's eyes and tries to conceive of one's existence corresponding to the feeling of 'I', one feels oneself to be a body. But that is a wrong idea. I am a spirit living in a body. The body will die but I shall not die. I have also a past which goes beyond the present body. The soul was not created, as creation implies combination and a sure and certain dissolution in the future. Again to hold that God is the creator of the soul will be tantamount to attributing partiality and cruelty to him, as He will be solely responsible for the unequal distribution of enjoyments and sufferings we meet in the world. Next, the idea of a creator does not explain the anamolies of life but simply expresses the cruel fiat of an all-powerful being. So there must have been causes before birth to make a man miserable or happy, and those are his past actions.

It may be argued against this that inherited aptitude is an adequate explanation, and that matter and its transformation

are sufficient to explain everything in life, and there is no
necessity for accepting the existence of a soul. "But it
cannot be proved that thought has been evolved out of matter,
and if a philosophical monism is inevitable, spiritual monism
is certainly logical and no less desirable than a materialistic
monism; but neither of these is necessary here." It is no
doubt true that cerain tendencies are acquired by heredity,
but that only means the physical configuration through which
a peculiar mind alone can act in a peculiar way. But heredity
fails to give an adequate explanation for various other tendencies and capacities of the individual as also to give the moral
grounds for the sufferings and enjoyments of life. All that
can be said about heredity is that "a soul with a certain tendency would by the laws of affinity take birth in a body which
is the fittest instrument for the display of that tendency." As
repetition is necesssary for explaining habits, we have to
assume a previous life to account for the natural habits of a
new-born individual. Still a question arises how it is that
we do not remember anything of the past life. The answer
is that even in this life not all our experiences are within the
purview of our memory. "That shows that consciousness
is only the surface of the mental ocean and within its depths
are stored all our experiences. Try and struggle, they would
come up and you will be conscious of even your past life....
Verification is the perfect proof of a theory, and here is the
challenge thrown to the world by the Rishis. We have
discovered the secrets by which the very depths of the ocean
of memory can be stirred up. Try it and you would get a complete reminiscence of your past life."

So according to a Hindu the real man is a spirit whom
the sword cannot pierce, fire burn, water wet, nor the air dry.
"Every soul is a circle whose circumference is nowhere, but
whose centre is located in the body, and death means

change of this centre from body to body. Nor is the soul bound by the conditions of matter. In its very essence, it is free, unbounded, holy, pure and perfect, but somehow or other it finds itself tied down to matter and thinks of itself as matter."

Now the question will be asked how and why the perfect spirit thus comes to be limited by matter. Some say that the Hindu shirks such a question and says that no such question can be there. But the Hindu is sincere and honest and admits, "I do not know it, I do not know the why of that question." But the fact is a fact for all that, felt in the conciousness of all. That it is the will of God, is no more an explanation than telling, 'I do not know.'

Doctrine of Isvara

Thus the human soul is eternal and immortal, perfect and infinite, and death means only a change of centre from one body to another. The actions of the past embodiment will manifest in the nature of tendencies of the present body, and the present, of the future. Thus the soul will go on evolving up or reverting back from birth to death and death to death. But then the question arises: Is man, a tiny helpless victim of an inexorable current of cause and effect, irresponsive to his weal and woe? The heart sinks at such an idea and yet this is the law of Nature. To the agonised heart of man, yearning for a way out of it, came the words of hope and consolation in the word of a Vedic Rishi who proclaimed the glad tidings: "Hear ye children of immortal bliss!..........I have found the ancient One, who is beyond all darkness and delusion. Knowing Him alone, you shall be saved from death over again." Thus the Vedas give the assurance that you are not sinners doomed to destruction but the sharers of immortal bliss, blessed and blissful and eternal—that you are not a mere combination of matter, but matter is your servant and not you of the matter. Further, the Vedas assure us that Reality is not a dreadful combination of unforgiving laws nor an endless prison of cause and effect, but in and through every particle of matter, stands One "by whose command the wind blows, the fire burns, the clouds rain and death walks upon the earth."

And what is His nature? "He is everywhere, the pure and formless one, the Almighty and the all merciful." He is our father, mother and beloved friend. He is the source of our strength, and it is He who takes the burden of this universe and also helps man to bear the little burden of his life. And how is He to be approached and worshipped? Through love, as one beloved, dearer than everything in this and the next life.

Sri Krishna's doctrine of Love and Non-attachment

This doctrine of love declared in the Vedas was fully developed and taught by Krishna who the Hindus believe to be God incarnate. In the first place he taught that man must live in the world like a lotus leaf, which grows in water but is never moistened by water—his heart to God and his hands to work. Further he taught the doctrine of motiveless love of God. God should be loved not for the rewards one expects of Him but with a love that seeks nothing except the privilege of loving. One of his disciples, Yudhishthira, the then emperor of India, was ousted by his enemies from the throne and banished to the forests. When questioned by his queen, why he should be devoted to God who did not save him from disaster, Yudhishthira answered: "Behold, my queen, the Himalayas! How grand and beautiful they are! They do not give me anything, but my nature is to love the grand, the beautiful; therefore I love them. Similarly I love the Lord, the source of all beauty and and sublimity....I do not pray for anything of Him. Let Him place me wherever He likes. I must love Him for love's sake. I cannot trade in love."

Doctrine of Mukti or Liberation

The Vedas thus teach the soul to be divine, only held in the bondage of matter. It will be restored to perfection when this bond is burst. The state that follows is called Freedom, Mukti,—freedom from the bonds of imperfection, from the sway of death and misery. This liberation from bondage can come only through the mercy of God, and this mercy comes to the pure. To the pure in heart He reveals Himself even in this life, and then only all doubts will cease, all the crookedness of the heart get straightend and freedom from the fear of the terrible law of causation cease to operate. This is the very centre, the very vital teaching of Hinduism— that a purified aspirant, the receipient of divine grace can have the direct understanding of the spiritual verities like Atman (soul) and Brahman (God). Thus the Hindu religion consists not in believing certain doctrines or dogmas but in realisation, "in being and becoming". One who attains the state of perfection enjoys eternal bliss with God.

The Advaitic Development of the above Doctrines

So far all sects of Hindus are agreed in their view, but the doctrine of Advaita goes a step further. Perfection, according to the Advaita, is the Absolute and the Absolute cannot be two or three. It cannot have the difference of substance and qualities. It cannot be an individual. So when the soul becomes perfect, it must become one with Brahman, the Absolute. "It must realise the Lord as the perfection, the reality of its own nature and existence, the Existence-Knowledge-Biiss Absolute." This state is often misrepresented as "the losing of individuality and becoming a stock or a stone." This is a gross misrepresentation. "If it is happiness to enjoy the consciousness of this small body, it must be greater happiness to enjoy the consciousness of two bodies, the measure of happiness increasing with the consciousness of an increasing number of bodies—the aim, the ultimate of happiness, being reached when it would have become the universal consciousness." So to get this individuality, this miserable little prison individuality must go. Misery can cease only when you are one with happiness, ignorance can cease only with the gaining of oneness with knowledge. This attainment of oneness is the only scientific religion we can have. For science is nothing but the discovery of unity underlying all multiplicity and all duality of experienced phenomena.

The Truth about Image Worship

Now coming down from religion enlightened by the aspirations of philosophy to the religion of the masses, it must first be understood that there is neither polytheism nor idolatry in India. In every temple in India, you will find the worshippers applying all the attributes of God including omnipresence to the images. A tree is known by its fruits. "When I have seen amongst them that are called idolaters, men, the like of whom in morality and spirituality and love I have never seen anywhere, I stop and ask myself: 'Can sin beget holiness?' Superstition may be a great enemy of man but bigotry is worse." It is only bigotry on the part of the image-destroying religionists to accept the holiness of their own images and places of worship while condemning those of the Hindus. To these critics 'omnipresence of God' means nothing more than a word or a symbol. They may at the utmost associate with it the idea of the extended sky or space.

Just as our mental constitution compels us to associate our idea of infinity with the image of the blue sky or with ,the sea, we naturally connect our ideas of holiness with the image of a church, a mosque or a cross. The Hindus, for their part, associate these and other ideas with different images and forms. Onlythere is this difference.While these critics of imageworship remain stagnant, giving intellectual ascent to such doctrines, the Hindu worship of images is a step, a half-way house, towards realisation. In Hinduism external worship is the first step, next is mental prayer, and finally there is the realisation of the Lord. The same Hindu kneeling before an image tells: "Him the sun cannot express, nor the moon, nor the stars, the lightning cannot express Him, nor what we speak of as fire; through Him they shine."The main difference between the image worship of the Hindus and that of their critics is this: the Hindus do not abuse the other's image or call his worship a sin. "To the Hindu, man is not travelling from error to truth, but from truth to truth, from lower to higher truth. To him all religions, from the lowest fetichism to the highest absolutism, means so many attempts of the human soul to grasp and realise the Infinite........and each of these marks a stage of progress; and every soul is a young eagle soaring higher and higher, gathering more and more strength till it reaches the Glorious Sun."

The Harmony of Religions

To the Hindu, the whole world of religions is only travelling to the same goal. "Every religion is only evolving a God out of the material man, and the same God is the inspirer of all of them." If they contradict one another in some respects, "the contradictions come from the same truth adapting itself to the varying circumstances of different natures." It is the same light coming through glasses of

different colours. The consequence of this universalism of
the Hindu outlook is that "throughout the whole system of
Sanskrit philosophy, there is no such expression as that the
Hindu alone will be saved and not others."

Universality of Hinduism

The Buddhists and Jains do not depend upon God
but the aim of their religions is to evolve a God out of man.
"They have not seen the Father, but they have seen the Son.
And he that has seen the Son has seen the Father also."

Thus it will be seen that Hinduism is the most universal
of all the religions. It is infinite like the God it preaches—
that is, it "will not be Brahminic or Buddhistic, Christian or
Mohamamden but the sum total of all these and still have
infinite scope for development." In its catholicity it will embrace
in its infinite arms, and find a place for, every human being—
from the grovelling savage to the man of spiritual enlightenment. It will have no place for persecution and intolerance
in its polity. It will recognise the divinity in every man and
woman, and its whole scope and force will be centred in
aiding to realise its own true divine nature.

It was reserved for America to proclaim to all quarters
of the globe that the Lord is in every religion. "May He,
who is the Brahman of the Hindus, the Ahura-Mazda of the
Zoroastrians, the Buddha of the Buddhists, the Jehovah of the
Jews, the Father in heaven of the Christians, give strength to
you to carry out your noble idea."

Address at The Final Session

My thanks to those noble souls whose large hearts and
love of truth had dreamed this wonderful dream and then
realised it. Much has been said of the common ground of
religious unity. This unity cannot come by the triumph of

any one of the religions and the destruction of the others. It can come only by every religion assimiliting the good points in other religions. "The Christian is not to become a Hindu or a Buddhist, nor a Hindu or a Buddhist to become a Christian; but each must assimilate the spirit of the others and yet preserve his individuality and grow according to his own law of growth. If the Parliament of Religions has shown anything to the world, it is this: It has proved to this world that holiness, purity and charity are not the exclusive possession of any church in the world and that every system has produced men and women of the most exalted character." On the banner of every religion, will soon be written 'Help and not fight', 'Assimilation and not destruction', 'Harmony and Peace and not Dissension.'

ON HINDUISM*

India as the Punya Bhumi

The little success that has attended my work in the West is not due to any inherent power of mine, but due to the good will and cheers that have been showered on me from our sacred motherland. This idea that our land is a sacred place, a Punya-bhumi, was a traditional belief with me, but having seen the world at large and the life of people in other parts of the world, what was a mere belief has now become a firm conviction. If there is any land to which all souls on this earth must come to account for their Karma and attain their last birth before salvation,—the land where humanity has attained its highest towards gentleness, generosity, purity and calmness, and above all, the land of introspection and spiritu- ality,—it is India. In the past, from here have proceeded great ideas of religion and waves of spirituality to all the surrounding countries, and in future, too, the wave that is going to spiritua- lise the materialistic civilisation and quench the burning fire of materialism in other parts of the world, has to originate in India.

Comparing country with country, there is no other race on this earth to which the world owes so much as to the mild Hindu. The term 'mild Hindu', used as a term of reproach, conveys a wonderful truth about our national life. Great ideas have gone from several ancient people like the Greek, the Romans, the Persians etc., as also from modern nations. But it was as a camp-follower of their conquering armies that the ideas contributed by them have penetrated into different countries. But we have never been a conquering race,

*Vol. III, p. 104. Delivered at Colombo.

ON HINDUISM

carrying fire and sword to helpless people vanquished in war. And therefore we have survived in the world as a nation during these several millennia in spite of foreign conquests and subjection, while those nations depending on military might have passed away long ago after a short period of meteoric existance of exultant and exuberant dominance and of a wicked national life.

Religion as the Prime Concern in India

What is the secret of this strength? Believe me when I say, after my experience of the world, it is here. "To the other nations of the world, religion is one of the many occupations of life, and among all these various occupations of life, there is perhaps a bit of religion. But here in India religion is the one and the only occupation in life." This has been the case with us for the past several millenniums, and as a consequence our culture and national genius have derived a special bent or direction in which alone they are bound to travel now and in the future also. Each race, by virtue of its past, has such a bent, a peculiar *raison d'etre*, and a particular mission to fulfil in the life of the world. Political greatness or military power has never been the mission of our race. But there has been the other mission given to us, which is to conserve, to preserve, to accumulate, as it were, into a dynamo, all the spiritual energy of the race, and that concentrated energy is to pour forth in deluge on the world, whenever circumstances are propitious. Let the Persian or the Greek, the Roman or the Arab, or the Englishman march his battallions, conquer the world, and link the different nations together, and the philosophy and spirituality of India is ever ready to flow along the newly made channels into the veins of the nations of the world. The Hindu's calm brain must pour out its own quota to the sum-total of human progress. India's gift to the world is the light spiritual.

The Need of India's Spiritual Ideals in the West

This has happened several times in the past when conquering nations linked the distant parts of the world by the lines of communication they established. It is happening today also when the world has been linked more closely than ever. Referring to the flooding of the world with Indian spiritual ideas that is silently taking place, the German philosopher Schopenhauer foretold: "The world is about to see a revolution in thought more extensive and more powerful than that which was witnessed by the Renaissance of Greek literature." This prediction is now coming to pass.

The effect of Indian thought and literature on the mind of men of alien civilisations is one of fascination. It is the opposite of anything that takes one suddenly. On the other hand it throws on you a charm imperceptibly, which gradually overcomes the sense of alienness and repulsiveness felt at first and exercises an abiding influence on the mind. "Silent and slow, as the gentle dew that falls in the morning, unseen and unheard, yet producing a tremendous result, has been the work of this calm, patient, all-suffering, spiritual race upon the world of thought."

To the observers of the trends of world-thought, this will be evident. Modern scientific criticism is giving a death blow to all narrowness, to all fanatical dogmatism in the West. Modern theories like conservation of energy, evolution etc. are making it impossible for cultured minds to accept the crude theologies that held sway in the world in the past. The vacuum that is thus being created can be filled only by broad, rational and ennobling ideas, and these are "only to be found in that most marvallous product of the soul of man, that wonderful voice of God, the Vedanta."

Laws, Eternal and Temporary

When I speak of the thought of India penetrating into other parts of the world, I mean only the broad underlying principles of the Vedanta, and not the code of customs and and manners developed in the course of centuries according to the social needs of the times. Indian tradition recognises two sets of truth. One set consists of the eternal verities dealing with the nature of man, the truth of God or Isvara, the relation of the Jiva to Isvara, the cyclic theories of creation, the doctrine of rebirth etc. Then there is the other set of rules and regulations dealing with society and daily lives of men. These are included in what are called the Smritis and they have application for the time and place to which they refer, and are not of universal importance. But the other set of truths, "the great underlying principles, being based upon the eternal nature of man, are as potent today for working for the good of the human race, as they were thousands of years ago, and they will remain so, as long as this earth remains, so long as the law of Karma remains, as long as we are born as individuals and have to work out our own destiny by our individual power."

The Ideal of Universal Acceptance

Above all, what the world needs from India is the idea of the harmony and acceptance of all religions, so that fanaticism and religious wars may not mar the life of man and the progress of civilisation. In the ancient world outside India, among the Babylonians and the Jews, each tribe had a god known under the generic name of Baal and Moloch respectively.

When the tribes fought among themselves for domination, the victor also displaced the Baal or Moloch in the temple of the vanquished with its own god. Thus Baal-Merodach was the greatest god among Babylonians, and Moloch-Yahveh among the Jews. The supremacy of gods was thus settled by battle.

In India, however, religious evolution took another turn. Here also there were several gods, but it was realised early in the Vedic times itself that Truth or God is one, but sages call Him differently. This idea gained strength in India with the progress of life and civilisation, and became the bedrock of the great Indian ideal of universal acceptance in contrast with the western idea of toleration in religious matters. In the light of the Indian tradition, it is the same God that different cults worship under different names and forms. "It is not that Siva is superior to Vishnu, nor is it that Vishnu is everything and Siva is nothing, but it is always the same One whom you call either Siva or Vishnu or by a hundred other names. The names are different but God is the same one."

As a consequence of this doctrine, there has been very little of religious persecution in India, whereas in regard to other parts of the world, their history is replete with religious wars. Even now there is very little of true religious toleration in the West. They may talk of it, but the orientation of their religion makes it impossible for them to practise it. "There is tremendous religious persecution yet in every country to which I have been and the same old objections are raised against learning anything new. The little toleration that is in the world, the little sympathy that is yet in the world for religious thought, is practically here, in the land of the Aryas, and nowhere else. It is here that Indians build places of worship for Mohammedans and Christians, nowhere else......

The one great lesson that the world wants most, that the world has yet to learn from India, is the idea not only of toleration, but of sympathy. Well has it been said in the *Mahimnah-stotra*: "As different rivers, taking their start from different mountains, running straight or crooked, at last come into the ocean, so, O Siva, the different paths which men take through different tendencies, various though they appear, crooked or straight, all lead unto Thee." This means that we must understand and accept that all worship is given to the one God, whatever be the name or the form; that all knees bending towards the Caaba or kneeling in the Christian church or in a Buddhist temple, are kneeling to Him, whether they know it or not.

Differentiation is the law of life, and religious differences are bound to persist, but it does not mean that we should hate each other. This can be achieved only if the Truth of universal acceptance preached in India from times immemorial is preached all the world over. There are many other lessons that the world can learn from India, but they are for the learned.

VEDANTISM*

The Scriptures of Hinduism

The word Hindu is a meaningless expression. It merely means those who lived on the other side of the river Indus (in Sanskrit *Sindhu*). The ancient Persians murdered the word into Hindu, meaning those who lived on the other side of Sindhu. During the period of Muslim domination, we took up the word ourselves, and it has continued to this day. But today it is meaningless, as various religionists live in India. The more appropriate name for us will be Vaidikas or followers of the Vedas, or better still Vedantists or the followers of the Vedanta.

Just as all religionists have a scripture, the Hindus or the Vedantists have the Veda as their scripture. The Veda, according to us, is not written by any man, but is eternal as creation itself. While the scriptures of all other religions owe their authority to certain personages, the Veda is self-existent, being the knowledge of God, without a beginning or an end. It was discovered by certain great personages called the Rishis, but never composed by them.

This mass of sacred literature called the Veda is divided into two parts, the Karma-Kanda and the Jnana-Kanda—the work portion and the knowledge portion, the ceremonial and the spiritual. The work portion consists of ceremonials like sacrifices, and it has mostly been given up as not practicable under the present circumstances. But the Jnana-Kanda or the spiritual portion, which comprises the Upanishads, also called the Vedantas, holds good to this day. Vedanta, literally meaning the end of the Veda, gives us the gist, the

---

*Vol. III, p. 116. Delivered at Jaffna.

essence and the goal of the Vedic teachings. All Hindu philosophies and sectaries accept the Upanishads or the Vedantas as their supreme authority with freedom to interpret it in their own way. The teachings of the Upanishads have gone so deep into our race that they emerge in the everyday life of the Hindu in the shape of symbols used for worship.

Next to the Vedanta comes the Smritis in the scale of scriptural authority. They deal mainly with the manners, customs, practices and forms of worship. These texts are composed by certain sages for certain times and for certain people. They can therefore change from age to age and time to time, but not so the main principles of religion regarding the nature of the Deity, the nature of the human spirit, the life hereafter, the goal of spiritual perfection etc., which form the themes of the Upanishads and the Srutis.

Then there are the Puranas which were written in simple Sanskrit, illustrating and expounding the philosophy of the Upanishads. They were meant for ordinary people who could not understand much of philosophy. The Puranas explain this philosophy in concrete form by means of the lives of saints and kings and great men and historical events that had a significant effect on the lives of the people.

There are still other books called the Tantras. They are very much like the Puranas in many respects, and in some of them there is an attempt to revive the sacrificial ideas of the old Karma-Kanda.

All these constitute the scripture of the Hindus. They are all valid to the extent that they do not contradict the Veda.

Essential Points common to all Hindus:
Theory of Creation

When there are so many scriptures evolved through the

course of several millenniums, it is natural that there will be several sects, but there are many common points on which they agree. These form the essential principles of Hinduism.

The first of these principles is the theory of creation. Creation does not mean that God suddenly brought out the world out of nothing. The meaning of the Sanskrit word Srishti is not creation but projection. Nature, Prakriti or Maya, the stuff of creation, is eternal and God is eternally creating, supporting and dissolving this stuff in a cyclic manner. Nature is now in a manifested form with multifarious world systems. After a period of manifestation it gradually dissolves into the original state of fineness, but again comes into manifestation after a long period of quiescence. This goes on eternally as a cyclic motion. Time, space and causation are within it, and to ask when it began is nonsense. The beginning of creation means only the beginning of a cycle.

Doctrine of God

Who is it that activates, sustains and withdraws this cosmic process? Brahman is the general cause of this manifestation. He is eternal, eternally pure, eternally awake, almighty, all-knowing, all merciful, omnipresent, formless and partless. But then a difficulty arises. We see partiality and cruelty in this creative process, for we find grave inequality in the distribution of enjoyment and suffering, and we find death as the necessary corollary of life. How is it compatible with the idea of a beneficent God? The Vedanta explains this by pointing out that the wind of God's mercy is always blowing, but many Jivas do not take advantage of it. The blame is not on God but on us. Besides, the distribution of happiness and misery depends on one's own doings or Karma, not necessarily now but in past births during the Jiva's long progress through Samsara.

The Doctrine of the Atman

The next question is, what is the soul? The ideas of soul and God are closely interconnected. All attempts at understanding the nature of the Infinite through external Nature are a failure. The study of external Nature does not help us very much to understand what is beyond Nature. The more we handle the material world, we seem to lose even our little spirituality. It is only the study of the internal nature, namely the analysis of the human soul, that can help us understand God. There are various ideas regarding the soul but in one respect all these views agree on the point that immortality, purity, omnipresence and omniscience are potential in each soul. The difference between souls is not in their essential nature but in manifestation. Because of this idea of sameness of all souls, India has stood for the brotherhood of all living creatures.

In Western philosophy and thought what they mean by soul is only the mind. They got the idea of the soul in the real sense only after they came into contact with Indian thought. So to prevent confusion it is better to designate the spiritual essence in man as the Atman. It is translated into modern language as the Self. The Atman is separate from the mind and body. Clothed in the mind or a mental body called Sukshma Sarira, the Atman goes from birth to birth through different physical embodiments until the Atman manifests the perfection that is within it and gains freedom. In the course of these embodiments, the Sukshma Sarira may go to other heavenly regions. These heavens are only the repetitions of this world with a little more of enjoyments. Those who attain to them by good works are again born on earth at the expiry of their merits. The attainment of the human body is a greater blessing because, while in heavenly embodi-

ments one is overpowered by ejoyments, here as man
the Atman has an opportunity to attain to non-attachment
and Mukti or freedom.   Even in the highest heaven, the Atman
is a slave—slave to happiness, space and time. "Nature
must fall at your feet and you must trample on it and be free
and glorious by going beyond. That alone constitutes Bliss
indestructible. What we call happiness and good here are but
particles of it."

How did the soul come into the present state of bondage?
There is but one answer, and that is, it is due to ignorance.
Knowledge can cure by taking us to the other side. "How
will that knowledge come? Through love, Bhakti. By the
worship of God, by loving all beings as the temple of
God."

The Personal and the Impersonal Ideas of God

There are two ideas of soul and God in our scriptures,
the Personal and the Impersonal. God as the Personal is the
omnipotent and omniscient creator, preserver and destroyer of
everything, the eternal Father and Mother of the universe. But
He is separate from the Atman. The Impersonal is without any
of these adjectives.   He cannot be thought of in human terms
and in relation to the Atman. He is one with it. This idea of
the Impersonal gives the best rationale of ethics.   The highest
ethical doctrine teaches that we must love all as ourselves.
Now the idea of the Impersonal God teaches the solidarity
of all life, the oneness of the universe and thus gives the reason
why you should love all.   Besides, it equips man with great
strength, because he is made to stand without any dependence—
in the glory of his own soul, the Infinite, the eternal and the
deathless. Thus all knowledge is in me, all power, all purity
and all knowledge.

The Doctrine of Ishtam

These are the principles of our religion. In their practice and application, many sects have been formed. But in the light of Vedantic teachings these sects do not claim any exclusive right over Truth to themselves and deny it to others. We have therefore the theory of Ishtam, the freedom to choose the path that suits us most. It is based upon the fact that different natures require different methods of worship and so it has been recognised from the most ancient times that there are various forms of worshipping God. For those who hold that there is only one path to God, it is absurd to talk of love of others. For, how can one who cannot bear another man to follow a different path from his own, love others? If that is love, what is hatred? So our attitude is, "If certain forms and formalities help you to realise the divine, God speed!" Thus our attitude is one of inclusion and not of exclusion.

In India caste and other social institutions are linked with religion. But really they have no inherent relation with it. They all came into being according to necessities of time and have changed from time to time. There is no meaning in totally condeming them if they have become antiquated. They have given some social stability through millenniums, which their modern critics are not able to secure. They can be changed, but it should not be made a ground for vilifying our past and our ancestors.

In this Kaliyuga, Dana or helping others is the most important form of spiritual practice. The highest form of Dana or gift is giving spiritual knowledge; next, giving secular knowlege; next, saving life, and last, giving food and drink. So the dissemination of spiritual knowledge contained in our great scriptures is one of the crying needs of our time. "But mere talking is not religion. We have to show it in a life

of renunciation and spirituality, of all-suffering and infinite
love. This kind of life indicates a spiritual man." Our
country abounded in such personalities embodying these great
qualities. Their life and ideas have to be placed before
India and the world at large. Work done in this direction is
also the best form of self-help. For, the more you help others,
the more you help yourself.

ADDRESS AT PAMBAN*

Spirituality as the Backbone of India

Our sacred motherland is a land of religion and philosophy—the birthplace of spiritual giants, the land of renunciation. Each nation appears to have a particular ideal—a prominent ideal running through its whole life, and this ideal is the backbone of its national life. Politics, military power, commercial supremacy, mechanical genius etc., are the fields of specialisation for different nations. But spirituality has always been the way of life in India.

It is widely thought that the Hindus are a mild and passive race, decadent and effete. This is an absurd notion. We have ever been spiritually active, and it is because of it that our most ancient and magnanimous race still lives.

The eyes of the whole world are now turned towards this land of India for spiritual food. Westerners are now striving to understand these ideals enshrined in Sanskrit. Religious research has discovered that there is not a country possessed of a good ethical code but has borrowed some of what it possesses, and there is not one religion having correct ideas of the immortality of the soul but has directly or indirectly drawn from us. We may be degraded and degenerated now, but however degraded and degenerated we may be, we can become great if only we begin to work in right earnes on behalf of our religion.

---

*Vol. III, p. 136. Delivered at Pamban.

REAL WORSHIP*

It is in love that religion exists and not in ceremony. Unless man is pure in body and mind, coming into a temple and worshipping Siva is useless. It is hypocrisy to be impure in life and yet try to preach religion to others. External worship is only a symbol of internal worship. Internal worship and purity are the only real things.

Many people think that in this Kali Yuga, they can go to holy Tirthas and wash away their sins. If a man goes to holy places and commits misdeeds there, he becomes all the more sinful. Thus it is most difficult to live in a Tirtha.

The gist of all worship is to be pure and to do good to others. "He who sees Siva in the poor and the diseased, really worships Siva; and if he sees Siva only in the image, his worship is but preliminary." Siva is more pleased with those who help his children than with those who praise Him. There are two gardeners, of whom one makes a show of respect and speaks highly of his master but remains lazy. The other does not do all these but produces an abundance of fruits and vegetables in the garden. With whom will the master be more pleased? So he who wants to serve Siva must serve His children. It is said in the Sastras that those who serve the servants of God are His greatest servants. By the power of such service, our heart becomes pure, and Siva, who is residing in everyone, will become manifest. Purity and unselfishness are the essence of spirituality, and he who has these, is nearer to Siva than those who are selfish in life, even though they might be regular in going to temples.

---

*Vol. III, p. 141. Delivered at the Rameswaram Temple.

INDIA'S GREAT SPIRITUAL MEN*

Spirituality, the foundation of India's national Life

The darkest days of India seem to be over. This mother-land of ours seems to be awakening from her deep, long sleep.

If my humble self has done some work in the cause of our religion and our motherland in Western countries, if my humble work has helped in rousing the interest of our people in the invaluable jewels that are lying buried in their own home — if anything has been accomplished towards these ends, India and the whole world owe much of it to you, the Raja of Ramnad, who passionately urged me towards this work, and helped and encouraged me all along. This our motherland is a land of philosophy, of spirituality and of ethics, of sweetness, gentleness and love. My experience of the world makes me bold to say that India is still the first and foremost of all the nations of the world in these respects. It is because of the interest of the people of this country in these matters that the very masses who are considered ignorant and wanting in desire for information about world politics, have come to know of the success of a Sannyasin at the Parliament of Religions and have got enthused about it. Each nation has got its own peculiarity and individuality with which it is born. In it lies the backbone, the foundation or the bedrock of its national life. Religion and spirituality form that foundation and national backbone of India. The one note that fills the Indian atmosphere is renunciation, which forms the watchword of Indian religions. The present life is of five minutes; beyond is the Infinite, beyond this world of delusion. This continent is

---

illumined with brave and gigantic minds and intellects which
think even of this so called infinite universe as only a mud
puddle; beyond it, still beyond, they go. This going beyond
the phenomenal is the very soul of religion. The Characteristic of my nation is this transcendentalism· India still
lives as a nation in spite of the vicissitudes of centuries, because
it holds fast to this spiritual ideal. This fountain of spirituality has to overflow and flood the world to bring in new life
and ʼnew vitality to the West. India, no doubt, has learnt
many things from the West in·the field of organisation, ability
to handle power and application of science to the betterment
of life. "But if anyone preaches in·India the ideal of eating
and drinking and merry-making, if anyone wants to apotheo-
sise the material world...., he has no place in this holy land.
....God alone lives; the soul alone lives; spirituality alone
lives; hold on to that."

The Two Dangers Ahead

It is no doubt true that men are at different stages of
evolution, and according to their progress they require some
degree of enjoyments of the world before they become fit for
the life of renunciation. There is provision for it in our
scriptures, but for sometime past we did the mistake of
exclusively emphasising on renunciation. The poor man
requires many good things of the world, and let us take
lessons from the Western people how we could do this. But
there are two dangers facing us, the Scylla of old orthodoxy
and Charybdis of European materialism. We have to steer
carefully between them. While absorbing the Western
ways of improving life in this world we should never give up
our hold on the spiritual ideal, which represents the national
life and forms the backbone of India. If we do so, in three
generations we will become an extinct race, or the foundations

on which our national edifice is built will then be undermined and the result will be annihilation all round. Therefore, whether you believe or not in spirituality, for the sake of the nation's sustenance, you have to maintain your hold on spirituality. Keeping a hold on that firmly, we can stretch the other hand out and gain all we can from other races. If we do that, a wonderful, glorious future India will come— an India greater than she ever was. "On our work depends the coming of the India of the future. She is there ready, waiting. She is only sleeping. Arise and awake, and see her seated here on the eternal throne, rejuvenated more glorious than she ever was—this motherland of ours.

"The idea of God was nowhere else ever so fully developed as in this motherland of ours .... They have only clanish Gods. The God of the Jews, the God of the Arabs, and of such and such a race, and their God is fighting the Gods of the other races. But the idea of that beneficient, the most merciful God, our father, our mother, our friend, the friend of our friends, the soul of our souls is here and here alone."

VEDANTA AS THE IDEAL RELIGION*

I am anxiously waiting for the day when mighty minds will arise and go forth from India to the ends of the world to teach spirituality and renunciation—those ideas which have come from the forests of India and belong to Indian soil alone.

Two attempts have been made in the world to found social life   one of them on spirituality or transcendentalism, and the other one on materialism or realism. Curiously enough, it seems that at times the spiritual side prevails and then the materialistic side, in wave-like motion following each other. In God's dispensation, both these have their own purposes to fulfil.   When a spiritually oriented civilisation degenerates, it ends in the concentration of power and wealth in the hands of a few. Then society has to help itself, and materialism comes to the rescue. Thus in God's economy everything, good and evil, has its own place.

Today Europe, the centre of manifestation of the material energy, is in imminent danger if it does not turn to spirituality as the basis of life.   And the saving message the world requires is to be found in the religion of the Upanishads. The underlying doctrine of that philosophy is the belief in the Atman, the soul of man. The Atman is ever pure and perfect by nature. We can never lose our nature. Only it is hidden by ignorance or Avidya. Ignorance makes the nature of the Atman unmanifest. It is ignorance that makes the difference between the highest man and the lowest worm that crawls under your feet. Faith in your inherent nature as the Atman, is the source of all strength and goodness.

---

*Vol. III, p. 155. Address at Paramakudi.

That faith generates fearlessness; the absence of it owing to
ignorance is the source of all fear and misery. That inherent
nature of the Atman cannot in any way be destroyed. It
may be hidden but at last it will conquer and come out. All
that you are today is of your own making. You yourself
manufacture your bodies. Thus the responsibility of good
and evil is in yourself. "But at the same time our religion
does not take away from mankind the mercy of the Lord.
He stands beside the tremendous current of good and evil.
He the boundless is ever merciful, is always ready to help us
to the other shore, for His mercy is great and it always comes
to the pure in heart.   Thus if a man wants a Personal God to
adore, he can find here the noblest idea of a Personal God
such as were never attained anywhere else in the world. When
man wants to be a rationalist and finds   satisfaction only in
reason, it is also here that he can find the most rational ideas
of the Impersonal."

THE PATH OF PROGRESS FOR INDIA*

The appreciation you have shown for the little work I have done in the West is only an indication of the tremendous approbation that spiritual giantsthat are to come in future will get from the nation. India is a land of religion. "We are fated by divine Providence to play the spiritual note in this family of nations, and it rejoices me to see that we have not lost the grand traditions which have been handed down to us by the most glorious forefathers, of whom any nation can be pround." We should become active and dispel the idea that we have degenerated at all.

The complaint has just been made that European materialism has well-nigh swamped us. If it is so, the fault is our own. A large section of the country is Mohammedan and Christian. Why did it happen? Because we did not show sufficient sympathy and bestow any attention to the poor and the down-trodden. On the other hand, think of the last six or seven hundred years of degradation, when grown-up men by hundreds have been discussing for years whether we should drink a glass of water with the right hand or the left, whether the hands should be washed three times or four times, whether we should gargle five times or six! What can we expect from men who pass their lives in discussing such momentous questions like these and writing most learned philosophies on them. There is danger of religion becoming kitchen-based. We are neither Vedantists, nor Pauranics nor Tantriks. We are first and foremost 'don't-touchists'. Our religion is in the kitchen. Our God is the cooking pot and our religion is 'Don't touch me. I am holy.' This

---

*Vol. III, p. 164. Address at Manamadura.

state of affairs has to change. "Vyasa says that giving alone is the one work in this Kali Yuga, and of all gifts, giving spiritual life is the highest gift possible. The next gift is secular knowledge. The next, saving of the life of man, and the last, giving food to the needy. If we follow this law for twenty five years, all our problems will be solved."

ETERNAL AND CHANGING PHASES
OF RELIGION*

Being in Madura as the guest of the Raja of Ramnad, I must acknowledge my indebtedness to him for encouraging me to go to Chicago for representing Hinduism and for extending his support for the same.

If spirituality is lacking in one part of the world and at the same time it exists elsewhere, it finds its way to the place where it is needed and thus balances the inequality. It has been the destiny of India in the past to supply spirituality to the world. "She contributed it even long before the rise of Persian Empire; second time it was during the Persian Empire; third time during the ascendency of the Greeks; and now for the fourth time during the ascendency of the English." Just as Western ideas of organisation and scientific technique are penetrating into the East, so Indian spirituality and philosophy are flooding the lands of the West.

In India there is a tremendous revival of religion but we have to be careful to find our way between the Scylla of old superstitious orthodoxy and the Charybdis of European materialism. You can never become great by imitating the West. It is impossible to do so, just like turning a river flowing from the Himalayan glaciers backward. But we must, however, be careful not to confuse local customs with the real religion.

There are two sorts of truths found in our Sastras—one based on the eternal nature of man, that is, which deals with the eternal nature of God and soul; and the other with local conditions at particular times, social institutions of the period and so forth.   The first class is embodied in the Vedas and the second in the Smritis, Puranas etc. If the latter conflicts with the former, the latter has to be rejected.   So you have to remember that if some of the social customs have to be changed, you are not going to lose your religion. Such customs have always been changing. So as time rolls on, new Smritis will come, sages will come, and they will direct the society through better channels according to the necessities of the age. Let us therefore be progressive and at the same time be as faithful and conservative towards our traditions as Hindus. In plain words, we have to learn the distinction between the essentials and the non-essentials in everything. The essentials are eternal while the non-essentials have value only for the time, and if after a time they are not replaced by practices suited for the new age, they will become positively dangerous. But for this reason, we should not revile practices that are old and out of date; for, they have been instituted by some great men at some time to suit the needs of those times. So we must change them without reviling them.

MISSION OF VEDANTA*

Spiritual Orientation of Religion in India

The appreciation you have shown everywhere for the little work I have done in the field of religion is indicative of the trend of our nation's mind. Religion is a matter of special interest for the people of India. For thousands of years the religious ideal has been dominating India for good or evil. It has entered into our very blood. So even if one wants to divert the nation's attention from it, it would be only like trying to make Ganga go back to its icy source. You can work only under the law of least resistance, and this religious line is the line of least resistance in India. "This is the line of life; this is the line of growth and this is the line of well-being in India."

In other countries also there is religion. But for them it is nowadays only a fashion, just as it is to have a Japanese vase. They are interested in politics, social improvement—in one word, in this world—and God and religion come in quietly as helpers to attain that goal. Their God is "so to speak, the being who helps to cleanse and to furnish this world for them. That is apparently all the value of God for them." They have criticised the religion of the Hindus, because it has failed to make them a conquering race but has turned them other-worldly in outlook. We on the other hand claim that this is the very greatness of our religion. This little earthly horizon of a few feet is not that which binds the view of our religion. Our religion makes us understand that this universe itself is like a drop in the transcendent ocean, the glory of the soul. "Ours is the true religion because it

___

*Vol. III, p. 177. Address at Kumbhakonam.

teaches that God alone is true, that this world is false and fleeting, that all your gold is but as dust, that all your power is finite, and above all, because it teaches renunciation." Through renunciation is the way to the goal and not through enjoyment. The proof of this is that all the aggressive and powerful nations of the past have been effaced from the world while the so-called 'meek' Hindu, who never conquered others, has survived through all these millenniums. It has vitality enough to deluge the world with its ideas when the time is ripe.

In the West how much a man can possess is the motivation. Thus the pursuit of enjoyment and luxury becomes their primary aim. The evil of such an outlook is gradually coming to be recognised by some great thinkers of the West. They are weary of this competition, struggle and brutality of the commercial civilisation, and they are looking for something better. They are recognizing that political and social manipulation of human conditions cannot cure the evils of life. It is the change in the heart of man that is required for this. So they are eager for some new thought or new philosophy. They have, no doubt, Christianity—a good and glorious religion that has been only imperfectly understood. "The thoughtful men of the West find in our ancient philosophy, especially in the Vedanta, the new impulse of thought they are seeking, the very spiritual food and drink for which they are hungering and thirsting."

Vedanta as the True Universal Religion: Principle versus Personality

Nowadays champions of Christianity claim that it is the only universal religion. But we can claim for valid reasons that Vedanta alone can claim that distinction. For the validity of Christianity and similar religions is essentially based on the

claim to the historicity of their founders. This is a very
flimsy foundation. For if that historicity is doubted, the whole
edifice falls down. On the other hand, Vedanta is based upon
principles. The Rishis are only the discoverers of those
eternal principles. Just as God is Impersonal and yet Personal, our religion, though based on principles, has yet an
infinite scope for the play of persons. For which religion
gives you more incarnations, more prophets and seers?
And there is the wonderful theory of Ishta which gives you
the fullest and the freest choice possible among these great
religious personalities. But all these personalities are illustrations of the eternally true principles of the Vedas. "The
glory of Sri Krishna is that he has been the best preacher of
our eternal religious principles and the best commentator on
the Vedanta that ever lived in India."

The second claim of the Vedanta upon the attention of the
world is that it is in agreement with the conclusions of modern
scientific investigations of external Nature. From ancient
times, the Greek mind and the Hindu mind started on the
study of the external Nature and internal Nature respectively.
While the conclusions of material sciences of the West are
not in agreement with their religion, it is only through the
message of the Vedanta of the Hindus that religion could be
reconciled with science. Two such points to which I want to
draw your attention are the idea of the universality of religions
and the idea of oneness of things.

Harmony of Religions in India

To take the first of these, the ancient Babylonians and
the Jews were divided into tribes, each having its tribal gods,
known often under a generic name—Merodac among the
Babylonians and Moloch among the semitic Jews. When
the tribes fought, the victorious party destroyed the god of the

vanquished, and installed their own god in his place. In this sort of conflict, entailing a long period of bloodshed, the Moloch Yahveh of the Jews displaced all other gods. This is the origin of the boasted monotheism of Semitic religions. In India it is just the other way. There were many gods worshipped here. In place of fighting for the supremacy of one over the other, it was declared by a wise Vedic sage, "He who exists is One, the sages call Him variouusly." This is the basic feature of the Hindu religion, making it the source of all religious toleration. As a consequence of this understanding of the unity of all the divinities worshipped,there is no persecution in this country unlike in the West where even now hostility to other religions is widely practised.

Unity of Existence

The other idea that the world wants from us is the grand idea of the spiritual oneness of the world. It is well known that the Western scientists have established the oneness and solidarity of the whole universe, each individual in it being only a wave or wavelet in the midst of an infinite ocean of matter. Indian psychology has demonstrated long ago that the same is the case with the mind. Going a step further, the Vedanta has shown that there is but one soul throughout the universe. This infinite oneness of the soul is the eternal sanction for all morality, for through that only the brotherhood of all living beings can be established. Besides, this understanding that we are part and parcel of that one divine spirit is necessary for generating faith in oneself. Lack of this faith is the cause of degeneration of character in India. So this Advaitic doctrine has to be preached, and I am doing so "not in a sectarian sense but upon universal and widely acceptable grounds." For all Vedantic sects say that God is in every soul. Therefore the individual spirit is

divine. Only according to the dualists, this divinity within
is contracted and according to the Advaitins it is obstructed.
In practice it amounts to the same thing.

The Way for the Uplift of India

Violating this great principle of Vedanta, we have for centuries treated vast masses of people as loathsome and untouchable. All kinds of obscurantism are paraded for justifying this
national sin.   For the uplift of these degraded Indian masses.
a set of people called the social reformers have come into
being for several decades.   Their method is to condemn
everything that is Indian. That way no good is done.   What
is required is that this great Vedantic doctrine of inherent
divinity has to be placed before the masses of mankind.   We
have to declare: "Arise, awake from this hypnotism of
weakness.   None is really weak.   The soul   is infinite,
omnipotent and omniscient. Stand up. Assert yourself
and proclaim the God within you.   Do not deny Him . . . . . . O
ye modern Hindus! Dehypnotise yourselves. The way to
do that is found in your own sacred books . . . . Power will
come.   Glory will come.   Goodness will come.   Purity will
come, and everything that is excellent will come, when this
sleeping soul is roused to self-conscious activity."

Then there is the difficult and vexed question of caste and
social reformation. In place of reform what we want is growth.
Mere condemnation is no help in this matter.   The ideal of
our social system is to make everyone a Brahmana, a spiritual
man.   The solution of the caste question is not by degrading
those who are already high but by everyone fulfilling the
dictates of our Vedantic religion by our attaining spirituality.

"I must therefore conclude, reminding you of this fact
that this ship of our nation, O Hindus, has been usefully
plying here for ages. Today perhaps it has sprung a leak;

today perhaps it has become a little worn-out; and if such is
the case, it behoves you and me to try our best to stop the
leak....Be patriots, love the race which has done such great
things in the past....Remember always there is not in the
world any other country whose institutions are really better
in their aims and objects than the institutions of this land....
Therefore utter no words of condemnation: close your lips
and let your hearts open."

MY PLAN OF CAMPAIGN*

Some Critical Remarks

There are certain facts about my work in the West of which I have not till now spoken out but which I should do now, as my countrymen want to know about it. It is propagated by the Theosophists that it is they who paved the way for my success in the West. This is absolutely untrue. When I was in America, friendless and with little means, I approached an American leader of the Theosophical society for a letter of introduction. But he refused to oblige me unless I became a member of that society. After I gained some success in the Parliament of Religions and came to be invited by individuals and societies of America, the Theosophists tried their best to cry me down· They advised their members not to attend my lectures. They also joined the Christian missionaries who began to spread about me every kind of lie imaginable that human ingenuity can invent. They began a campaign of character assassination in order to oust me from every house and to make every friend of mine an enemy. It was also very strange that a countryman of mine, representing a reform movement, also joined in this work of vilification out of pure jealousy.

The social reformers also, through their Organ, tried to cry me down by describing me as a Sudra who had no right to become a Sannyasin. Though I challenge the validity of this criticism, I shall be glad to be called even a Pariah as I am a disciple of one—a Brahmana of Brahmanas—who cleaned even the houses of scavengers. The criticism of

*Vol. III, p. 207. Address at Madras.

these social reformers only reveals what orthodox Hinduism will do.

Criticism of Reformers and their Ways

I have to say a word about reform societies. I differ from their attitude to the problems of evil in society. I do not believe in reform, but only in growth. For about a century the voice of these reformers is heard, but what have they achieved except the creation of a body of vituperative literature? The zeal for reform generates fanaticism and there is no force greater than fanaticism for generating evil. There is no special meaning in condemning the social evils in Hindu society. Evils of similar kind exist in every society. What is required is love and sympathy and not mere condemnation and fanaticism. Growth and not reform should be our watchword. For creating social changes, revolutionary and disruptive methods are of little use. You have to educate the public opinion. A few intellectuals trying to solve the problems of their small groups is not reformation. You have to touch the life of the masses. Today it is the fashion to talk of Buddhism and Buddhistic agnosticism. "Little do such persons know that this degradation which is with us today has been left by Buddhism." Our ancient Acharyas like Sankara and Ramanuja knew this. They knew also that sudden changes cannot be accomplished. The only way left to them was slowly to bring the masses up to the highest ideal held forth by the existing religion. The fundamental doctrine of their religion is evolution, "the soul going towards the highest goal through all these various stages which are therefore necessary and helpful."

It has become a fashion for reformers to condemn worship of images. For what reason, it is difficult to understand, except that it has been condemned by some ancient

Jews. But they had their own idols and what they condemned were only the idols of other people. Sri Ramakrishna was a worshipper of God through images from beginning to end. If such personages can be produced through image worship, what justification have the reformers to condemn it? India never lacked reformers. Sankara, Ramanuja, Nanak, Chaitanya, Kabir etc. were all reformers. But theirs was not the method of our present day reformers who want to condemn and destroy. They said to the people that they were good, but they must be better. Thus evolution or growth from within is what is required—and not the imitation of other societies and the foisting of their institutions on Indian society.

How the Ancient Masters effected Changes

My plan is to follow the ideas of the great ancient Masters, with whatever changes are needed by the changed circumstances. Each nation, like each individual, has one special theme in its life—a theme which is the principal note around which every other note comes to form the harmony of its life. In one nation it may be political power, in another artistic life and so on. But in India, religion has been the keynote of the whole music of national life. If any nation throws off its national vitality, that is, the direction which has become its own through the transmission of centuries, then that nation dies, if it succeeds in the attempt. So if you succeed in throwing off religion from India to take up other themes like politics or social refinement as the centre of your national life, then extinction of the nation will be the consequence. To prevent this you have to vitalise your religion first, and subordinate everything else to it. "That intense faith in another world, that intense hatred for this world, that intense power of renunciation, that intense faith in God, that intense faith in the immortal soul—is in you. How

can you change your nature?" So every improvement
in India should be preceded by an upheaval in religion·
"Before flooding India with socialistic and political ideas,
first deluge the land with spiritual ideas." The great truths
confined in the Upanishads and the Puranas mut be broadcast
all over the land. Let the people hear it first and all who
help in this process are practising the highest form of gift,
namely the gift of spiritual ideas. The dissemination of
these spiritual ideas should not be confined to India but
embrace all parts of the world. This has been India's mission
from times immemorial. Some of you think that I am
the first Sannyasin to go out to preach in the West. It is not so.
Even in pre-Buddhistic times, Indian thought had travelled
to other parts of the world. Whenever any conquering race
linked parts of the world by roads and other means of communication, Indian spiritual ideas have found their way to
reach distant places. Today the English genius has linked the
religions of the world in a way that has never been done
before, and Indian spirituality has begun to pour forth its
gifts along these new channels. "That I went to America was
not my doing or your doing, but the God of India who is
guiding her destiny sent me and will send hundreds of such to
all the nations of the world."

Therefore, my plan is to start institutions in India to train
our young men as preachers of the truths of our scriptures in
India and outside India. "Men, men....believing young
men, sincere to the backbone, are wanted. People have been
told that they are nothing, and nothing they have become."
"Let them hear that they are the Atman, that even the lowest
of the low has the Atman within, which never dies and never
is born, whom the sword cannot pierce, nor the fire burn,
nor the air dry—immortal, without beginning or end, all
pure, omnipotent and omnipresent. Let them have faith in

themselves. It is the self-confidence born of such faith that makes the difference between man and man, and between great nations and weak nations." "Make your nerves strong. What you want is muscles of iron and nerves of steel. It is the man-making religion that you want. . . . It is the man-making education all round that you want. And here is the test of truth—anything that makes you weak physically, intellectually and spiritually, reject it as poison. There is no life in it. . . . It cannot be true. Trutn is strengthening, truth is purity, truth is all knowledge. . . . Go back to your Upanishads, the shining, the strengthening, the bright philosophy, far from all these mysterious things, all these weakening things."

The True Ideal of Patriotism

There is so much talk about patriotism. Three things are necessary for great achievements in this field. "First feel from the heart. . . . Feel, therefore, my would-be reformers my would-be patriots. Do you feel that millions and millions of the descendents of gods and sages have become next-door neighbours to brutes?. . . . Does it make you restless? Does it make you sleepless? Has it gone into your blood coursing through your veins, becoming consonant with your heart beats? Are you seized with that one idea of their misery, of ruin, and have you forgotten all about your name, your fame, your wives, your children, your property, even your own bodies? Have you done that? That is the first step to become a patriot, the very first step. Next instead of spending your energies in frothy talks, have you found any way out, any practial solution, some help instead of condemnation? Yet that is not all. Have you got the will to surmount mountain-high obstructions? Have you got the courage to stick to your path even if all-round ruin faces you? If you have these three things, each one of you will work miracles.

"I am afraid I am delaying you, but one word more. This national ship, my countrymen, my friends, my children—this national ship has been ferrying millions and millions of years across the waters of life....But today perhaps through your fault this boat has become a little damaged, has sprung a leak, but would you, therefore, curse it?....If there are holes in the national ship, this society of ours—we are its children let us go and stop the leaks. Let us gladly do it with our heart's blood and if we cannot, then let us die....Never condemn it, say not one harsh word against this society. I love it for its past greatness. I love you all because you are the children of gods, because you are the children of those glorious forefathers. I have come now to sit in your midst and if we are to sink, let us all sink together but never let curses rise up to our lips."

VEDANTA AND ITS APPLICATION TO
INDIAN LIFE*

Vedantism is Hinduism

The word Hindu applied to us is a misnomer. The ancient Persians used to call the river Sindhu as Hindu. The word afterwards came to be applied for all people living beyond the Sindhu or the Indus. But today many other religions are also living beyond the river Indus and thus the word Hindu has lost its original significance. It has today come to mean only the followers of the scripture called the Vedas. So every sect called Hindu today looks upon the Vedas as the scripture. The Veda has got two sections, the Karma Kanda and the Jnana Kanda, of which the former dealing largely with sacrifices and ceremonial has fallen into disuse at present. The Jnana Kanda as embodying the spiritual teachings of the Vedas is known as the Upanishads or the Vedanta. All Hindu sects, dualists, qualified monists or monists accept the authority of the Upanishads. So it is more appropriate to call the modern Hindus as Vaidikas or the Vedantists.

The Upanishads and their All-inclusiveness

There is sometimes a tendency to apply the term Vedantist only to the followers of the Advaita system. This is not correct. The qulified dualists and the dualists also respect the Upanishads in an equal measure as the Advaitins. This incorrect idea has arisen because the great Advaita teacher Sankara quotes almost exclusively from the Upanishads while the teachers of the other sects resort to a very great degree

*Vol. III, p. 228. Delivered at Madras.

to the Puranas and other Smritis for supporting their teachings.

There is a misconception that the Upanishads do not contain the idea of Bhakti. This is absolutely incorrect. There is enough of Bhakti in every Upanishad if you will seek for it. "But many of these ideas which are found fully developed in later times in the Puranas and other Smritis, are only in the germinal stage in the Upanishads."

These Upanishads are our scriptures. It is an accepted principle that wherever there is a difference between the Vedic authority and the Pauranika literature, Vedic teaching must prevail. But in spite of this understanding, there are innumerable customs and practices of purely local nature prevailing in our society having no authority in the Veda. But when this is pointed out, conservative scholars are accustomed to say that these must have existed in those portions of the Vedas which have become extinct now. For, various branches of the Veda were specialised by particular families and when those families became extinct, those branches of learning also came into disuse. It is said in Patanjali's Mahabhashya that the Sama Veda itself had a thousand branches, but we cannot trace many of these branches today.

Another difficulty in understanding the Upanishads is that the commentators have tortured the texts to yield whatever meaning they want. For they presume that their own philosophy, non-dualistic, qualified non-dualistic, or dualistic, is alone true. It was given to me to live with a man who was equally an ardent dualist and an ardent Advaitist, an ardent Bhakta and an ardent Jnani, at the same time. And living thus with this man, made me attempt to understand the Upanishads from an independent and better point of view than by blindly following the commentators, and in my opinion and in my researches I came to the conclusion that these texts are not at all contradictory. The texts are beautiful, ay, they are most wonderful and are not contradictory, but wonderfully harmonious, one idea leading up to the other. The one fact that I found is that in all the Upanishads they begin with dualistic ideas with worship and all that, and end with the grand flourish of Advaitic ideas.

The Upanishads also constitute a grand poetical literature. In other language the poets attempt to describe the Infinite in terms of space and muscular strength. The Upanishads avoid this. Through a kind of negative yet poetic language they paint the Infinite as beyond the ken of the senses. The teaching of strength and fearlessness is another feature of the Upanishads. If you accept the teaching that man is the immortal spirit which nothing can destroy, you rise above all fear and get established in true strength. The story of an old Indian sage laughing derisively at Alexander the Great when he threatened to kill him, is an illustration of the type of strength that the Upanishads can impart. Next the Upanishads are the one scripture which talks not of salvation but of freedom. The soul is by nature divine. The expression of the divinity is obstructed by barriers of ignorance . The way to overcome this barrier is by asserting the eternal purity and power of the Spirit, and not by dwelling on the idea of sin. "I have been criticised from one end of the world to the other as one who preaches the diabolical idea that there is no sin! But the descendents of these very men will bless me as the preacher of virtue and not of sin. I am the teacher of virtue not of sin. I glory in being the preacher of light and not of darkness."

The Upanishads as a Doctrine of Unity and Strength

The second great idea which the world is wanting from

our Upanishads is the solidarity of the universe. Today, through intercommunication, people of every country are coming to recognise that the people of other countries are also like themselves. In politics and sociology it is increasingly found that problems facing each nation are international and cannot be solved at a purely national level. Science has established that all matter is one mass in which you and I, the sun and the moon and everything else are but the names of different little whirlpools and nothing more. Mentally also we are only little whirlpools in the universal ocean of thought. All this is parallel to the Upanishadic idea of the one unchangeable, unbroken, homogeneous Atman.

If the world at large wants this idea of oneness, we in this country want it all the more; for in spite of the greatness of the Upanishads, the people of this country are deplorably weak in body and mind. This physical weakness is the cause of one third of our miseries. "First of all our young men must be strong.... You will be nearer to heaven through football than through the study of the Gita.... For you will understand Gita better with your biceps, your muscles, a little stronger. You will understand the mighty genius and the mighty strength of Krishna better with a little of strong blood in you. You will understand the Upanishads and the glory of the Atman better when your body stands firm upon your feet and you feel yourselves as men."

People often blame me that I preach only Advaitism. I am not the preacher of any 'ism'—Advaitism or dualism. I preach only the wonderful idea of the soul contained in the Upanishads—its eternal might, its eternal strength, its eternal purity and its eternal perfection. To believe that you are basically this Atman is real faith. In Western countries, though their religions teach them to be sinners, the people believe themselves to be strong. For example, "the English man believes he is born the lord of the world. He believes that he is great and can do anything in the world. If he wants to go to the sun or the moon, he believes he can, and that makes him great." But in spite of the great ideas contained in the Upanishads, we think of ouselves as weak. It is strength that we want now, and "the first step in getting strength is to uphold the Upanishads and believe I am the soul—me the sword cannot cut, nor weapons pierce; me the fire cannot burn; me the air cannot dry. I am the omnipotent and I am the omniscient." At present you are not able to rise to any high level, "simply because your blood is only like water, your brain is sloughing, your body is weak. You must change the body. Physical weakness is the cause and nothing else."

The Upanishads should be preached to all

The Upanishad in the past was only for the Sannyasin. Sankara made it available also for the householders. But it is in the Gita, the best commentary on the Veda, that it is made available for everyone in every occupation of life. In the Gita the truths of the Vedanta are laid bare for every man. The idea that one is the immortal Atman should permeate every strata of society. For "if the fisherman thinks that he is the Spirit, he will be a better fisherman. If the student thinks that he is the Spirit, he will be a better student."

To broadcast this great ideal of the Upanishads is the way of effecting real reform, and not by mere condemnation of existing society nor by assuming the role of a dictator to people. "Look upon every man, woman and everyone as God. You cannot help anyone, you can only serve; serve the children of the Lord; serve the Lord Himself if you have that privilege. If the Lord grants that you can serve everyone of his children, blessed you are; do not think too much of yourselves....Do it only as worship." "Bring light to the poor and bring more light to the rich, for they require it more than the poor. Bring light to the ignorant and more light to the educated, for the vanities of the educated are tremendous."

THE WORK BEFORE US*

The Greek and the Indian

The problems of life are becoming increasingly world-wide in their implications. Even one atom cannot move without drawing the whole world with it. Real progress is possible only collectively. For the past few centuries our country became degraded because we have not been moving in unison with this expanding process.

Two great nations born of the same race have been working in two different directions in the history of the world. These are the ancient Aryans of India and the Greeks of ancient days. Stimulated by the surroundings in which they lived, the Aryans of ancient India became introspective, and analysis of one's own mind became the great theme of their work. The Greek on the other hand, surrounded by a Nature that is more beautiful than sublime, directed his mind outward to the study of external Nature. As time went on, the Indian's preoccupation with the internal exercised a narrowing influence on the mind. In our literature and philosophy, the ornate and florid style came to take the place of symmetry of form and sublimity of conception. In religious matters, it degraded to the level of a kitchen-religion. The great principles of Vedanta came to be confined to a few Sannyasins, while the best men of the country concerned themselves with 'don't-touchism' and impurity and purity of food. Then came the foreign conquests, first of Moham-medans and next of the English. All foreign conquest is an evil but even in that there is a silver lining. England and the whole of Europe represent a civilisation that is Grecian

---

*Vol. III, p. 269. Delivered at Madras.

in its origin and development. So the English conquest of
India has brought together the minds of the ancient Greeks
and of the ancient Indian Aryans. The result of the English
conquest is that we are drawn out of our narrow shells and
forced to take a broader conception of life, which was the
conception of our own ancestors too.

Causes of India's Downfall

One of the most important causes of India's degradation
is that we have for the past few centuries worked against the
expanding process of life. We have got to learn many things
from other races and we have also got to give them many
things. This is possible only when you go out. "We cannot
do without the world outside of India. It is our foolishness
that we thought we could, and we have paid the penalty by
about a thousand years of slavery. Life is expansion, and if
you stand against it, you become decadent or you die. That
we have now begun to think of going out to learn from
others and to give our quota of offering to the geneal mass
of human knowledge, is a sign of our revival. It is the sign
of our recovery of the spirit of ancient India—that we have
begun to feel the need of sending representatives of our
culture to foreign lands with the gift of our rich traditions.
The gift of India, the gift of philosophy and wisdom and
spirituality—these do not require the support of conquering
armies. So in the process of India's expansion, we have
never been a conquering race and that is the greatest point
of greatness with us. The one characteristic of the Indian
thought is its resilience, its calmness. Indian literature at
first repulses a foreign student but as he goes on with his
studies, it fascinates him. Like the gentle dew bringing into
blossom the fairest of roses, Indian culture had in the past
stimulated the cultural life of people outside without indulging

in bloody wars and contests. The greatest of our ancient
thinkers have not even given their names to their writings
unlike the moderns.

Need for the Expansion of India's Spiritual Culture

But thoughts like merchandise require channels, roads
for their expansion. Whenever in the world's history conquering races have established communications between
different parts of the world, Indian thought also moved along
those lines and influenced the lives of people. Thus even long
before Buddhism, Vedanta had penetrated into China, Persia,
islands of eastern Archipelago etc. When the Greek conquest
established links between the East and the West, Indian
thought penetrated to those regions, and Christianity with
all its boasted civilisation is but a collection of little bits of
Indian thought. "Ours is a religion of which Buddhism with
all its greatness is a rebel-child and of which Christianity is a
very patchy imitation." With the growth of the British
Empire, a new era of inter-connection of continents has
begun and India has to fulfil its age-long function by allowing
its thoughts to flow to all parts of the world. "It is not only
that we want to revive our own country—that is a small
matter. I am an imaginative man and my idea is the conquest
of the whole world by the Hindu race." By the conquest of
the world I mean the conquest by religion and spirituality
and not conquest by armies. They will tell you that we had
better look to our homes first and then go to work outside.
"But I tell you that you work best when you work for others.
This very meeting is proof of how the attempt of enlightening
other countries with your thoughts is helping our own country,
for even one fourth of the effect that has been produced in
this country by my going to England and America would not
have been brought about had I confined my idea only to

India." Spirituality must conquer the West. Slowly they
are finding out that what they want is spirituality to preserve
them as nations. Now the question is where are the men who
are ready to sacrifice everything so that this message shall
reach every corner of the world. Heroic souls are wanted
to go abroad and help to disseminate the great truths of the
Vedanta.

What I mean by the conquest of the world by spiritual
thought is the sending out of the life-giving principles, not
the hundreds of superstitions that we have been hugging to our
breasts for centuries. They have to be weeded out of even our
soil. In India there is danger today from two types of people,
both well-educated. There is, on the one hand, men who
after drinking the cup of Western wisdom think that they
know everything and pooh-pooh our religion and philosophy
as mere child's prattle or superstition. There are others, on
the other hand, who try to defend every village custom and
every superstition by giving them scientific explanations—
people who think that our religion will perish if these local
practices and beliefs are done away with. Their idea of
religion is mystery-mongering, which is always a sign of
weakness. It is better for one to be an atheist than be a
follower of superstitions and a member of a secret society.

The Uniqueness and Harmony of Vedic Thought

The teachers of every religion are now putting forward
the claim that theirs is the universal religion of the world.
Probably no particular religion is ever going to have sway
over the whole world. But if there is a religion which can
claim to be that, it is only our religion and no other, because
every other religion depends on some person or persons.
All other religions are based on what they claim to be historical

personalities and they think that their strength lies in that. But they little realise that if the historicity of their founders is questioned the whole fabric tumbles to the ground. "Half of the lives of these great founders of religions has been broken to pieces and the other half is doubted seriously." "But the truth of our religion, although we have persons by the score, do not depend on them. The glory of Krishna is not that he was Krishna but he was the great teacher of the Vedanta....Thus our allegiance is to principles always and not to persons. Persons are the embodiments, the illustrations of the principles. If the principles are there, the persons will come by the thousands and millions....These principles of our religion are always the same, and it should be the life work of every one to keep them free from accumulating the dirt and dust of ages."

It is sometimes pointed out that in the Vedas there are various apparently contradictory ideas, some dualistic and others monistic. In the past our commentators have tried to solve this contradiction by interpreting all the texts either in the dualistic or monistic way, mostly by adopting the device of text-torturing. But today this method is out of date. The Vedas contain both dualistic and monistic conceptions, and both of them are necessary for the evolution of the mind. So long as you have a body, have the five senses and see the external world, we must have a personal God. Nature, individual soul and God form a triangle that go together. "But there may be times in the lives of sages when the human mind transcends, as it were, its own limitations, when man goes beyond Nature to a realm of which the Sruti declares 'Whence words fall back without the mind reaching it'...... Then and then alone flashes into the human soul the conception of monism—I and the whole universe are only Brahman, are one; and this conclusion you will find has not only been reached through knowledge and philosophy but through the power of love also."

There are therefore many stages in the development of the human spirit and there is no need for quarrels. We must remember that true religion does not consist in external practices, putting particular marks on the body, dressing in a particular way, or going to temples and churches. True religion is realisation. All the externals are but aids. But if a man identifies religion with these externals, they retard in place of helping his progress. Our religion therefore lays down distinctly and clearly that everyone who wants salvation must pass through the stage of Rishihood—must become a *Mantra-drashta,* must see God. All power is there within you. Stand up and express the divinity within you.

THE FUTURE OF INDIA*

Why We Should Think of The Past

India is the ancient land where wisdom made its home before it went to any other country. Its rolling rivers and its towering mountains represent, as it were, its greatness on the material plane. Its soil has been trodden by the greatest sages that ever lived. The highest ideals of religions and philosophy have attained their culminating point here. From here waves of spirituality have again and again rushed out and deluged the world. It is the land that withstood the shock of hundreds of foreign invasions, of hundreds of upheavals of manners and customs, and yet stands firmer than ever with its undecaying vigour and indestructible life.

I refer you to the past of India, because its future is to take shape from that background. Out of the consciousness of our past greatness, we must build an India yet greater than what she has been. Periods of decadence there have been, but out of these India emerged always as something greater, as a mighty tree from a decayed fruit.

The problems of India are more complicated than those of any other country. Here there are people of diverse races speaking a conglomoration of languages and following manners and customs of utmost diversity. The one common ground we have is our sound traditions, our religion. There must be the recognition of one religion throughout the length and breadth of this land. But it is not in the sense the Christians, the Mohammadans and the Buddhists think of religion. We have certain common grounds for all our sects and within their limitation our religion admits of a marvellous variation,

---

*Vol. III, p. 285. Delivered at Madras.

infinite amount of liberty to think and live our own lives. People must be made aware of those common grounds in the first place. In India we have, no doubt, various differences of race, linguistic difficulties, social differences etc. But they melt away before the unifying power of religion. Our religion has been the key-note of Indian life, and therefore it is the line of least resistance for work in India. The unification of religion, therefore, is the first step in the building up of future India. The dualists, the qualified monists, monists, Saivas, Vaishnavas etc., must give up all their little quarrels and differences which are really condemned by our scriptures and forbidden by our forefathers.

Solution of the Caste and Ethnic Problems

Our life-blood is spirituality. If it courses pure and strong and vigorous, everything will get right. If the disease germ is thrown out of the body, then the vitality of the body is reassured. In the same way when the national body is weakened, then all sorts of disease germs enter into the social, educational and political fields, crowd into the system and produce diseases. The source of the vigour of our national life has always been our religion. Whether you like it or not, you are bound by it in all our attempts of national regeneration. I do not mean to say that other aspects of life, social, political etc. are not necessary or important. I mean only to say that they are only secondary while religion is primary. So if religion, the primary factor of our national life, is strengthened, all other aspects of our life too will be invigorated.

I shall now place before you some ideas that I have in mind about this. The great spiritual ideals of India have in the past been hidden in the monasteries and much more in the Sanskrit language, unknown to the masses of the country. So first of all these spiritual ideas should be brought out in the language of the people. But at the same time, vigorous attempt must be made to popularise Sanskrit among the masses; for knowledge can be given through any language, but what is called culture can be imparted in India only through Sanskrit. Knowledge without culture is only skin-deep. So, for raising the masses, both these—the interpretations of the scriptures in the regional languages and at the same time propagation of Sanskrit—are necessary.

Next I want to discuss a problem that has special bearing on Madras. A theory has been propounded that there was a race of mankind in South India called the Dravidians and that in North India called the Aryans, and that the Brahmanas of the South are only the Aryans that came from the North. Various theories of the original home of the Aryans are propounded by scholars according to their particular fancies. They are all guess-works prompted by pure imagination. There is nothing to prove that the Aryans ever came to India from outside. So also is the theory that a few Aryans from the North settled down in the South and dominated over thousands of slaves. This is an impossibility. The only explanation of these differences is what is found in the Mahabharata that in the beginning of the Satya Yuga there was only one Varna, that of the Brahmana, and then by differences of occupations they went on dividing themselves into different castes. In the Satya Yuga that is to come, all these Varnas have to go back to the same original condition. So the solution of the caste problem in India assumes this form, not to degrade the higher caste but to raise everyone to the state of Brahmanahood. The Brahmana, the man of God, one who has the knowledge of the Veda, must remain. But he has no claim for any exclusive privilege as a closed community. The days of such exclusive privileges are gone under the British rule. It is this claim for exclusive privileges by the well-placed castes that drove a fifth of our countrymen to become Muslims, and another fifth is going to become Christians if the invidious distinctions of privileges is not done away with. In the past also this process of up-lifting lower caste to higher has been effected by the great Acharyas like Sankara, Ramanuja and others. Hordes of Baluchis and Tartars were made into Kshatriyas, and a number of fishermen into Brahmanas.

This dispute and conflict between castes must cease because they weaken the nation. He only is a Brahmana who has no secular employment. It is the duty of the Brah-manas of India to remember what real Brahmanahood is. "As Manu says, all these privileges and honours are given to Brahmanas, because with him is the treasury of virtue." The other castes must remember that if they remain back-ward, it is only because they sat down lazily and let the Brahmanas win the race. But it is one thing to gain an advan-tage, and another thing to reserve it for misuse. The Brah-mana was only the trustee of the culture. He must have imparted it to the people at large, and it was because he did not do this that the Mohammedan invasion was possible. To the underprivileged I say, "Why do you fret and fume because somebody else has more brains, more energy, more pluck to go ahead than you?" Instead of wasting their energies in quarrels, let them absorb the culture of the Brahmanas, and this will take place if all people take to Sanskrit education, because Sanskrit and prestige go together in India.

The Way to build up our Future

The future of India depends entirely upon all its people working together with one will. Power is gained only through the concentrated will of a group of people. That is how small nations with united will have been able to dominate over vast masses of men, all divided among themselves. If all the dissensions based on the caste are allowed to continue, we as a nation cannot become strong.

The worship of the Virat is the greatest need of the times. The Virat is the manifested universe. For us our own country and our countrymen are the Virat. These we have to worship, instead of being jealous of each other and fighting with each other. Such worship brings about Chitta-suddhi or purification of the heart.

We must have a hold on the spiritual and secular education of the nation. The education that we are now getting may have some good points, but its defects outweigh. Then, it is entirely negative in its nature. It teaches that all your ancients were worthless men and that our past is a blank. The system of such education for the past fifty years has not created any original men. In place of it, we want a man-making education. "Education is not the amount of information that is put into your brain to remain there undigested all your life. We must have life-building, man-making, character-making assimilation of ideas." If you have assimil-ated five ideas and allowed them to enter and mould your life and character, you have more education than any man who has got by heart a whole library. This is a very big scheme that has to be properly planned.

THE SAGES OF INDIA*

Vedanta gives Precedence to Principles over Personailties

The Hindu nation has been producing sage after sage during the thousands of years of its existence. But these sages or great incarnations are not the originators of our religion. They are only the exemplars and expounders of its truth. Our religion has got two sets of scriptures— the Sruti and the Smriti. The Sruti or the Veda deals with eternal principles like the nature of the soul, the relationship between souls, the nature of God and His relationship with the soul etc. The Smritis are compositions of men like Manu and Yajnavalkya. There are also the Puranas and the Tantras. They work out the details of the principles laid down in the Vedas and deal with the lives of great personalities who have exemplified them. But it must be remembered that the principles contained in the Veda do not derive their authority from any personality, unlike the teachings of other religions. Personalities are great according to the thoroughness with which they embody the principles of the Veda. Our first principle is that all that is necessary for the perfection of man and for attaining the freedom is there in the Vedas. There is nothing new to be added to it, for when *Tat Tvam Asi* was discovered the spiritual science reached perfect unity which is the goal of all religions. The work of the great teachers is only to guide the people in varying circumstances and environments and according to time and place on the lines laid down in the Vedas. The eternal principles stand upon their own foundations without depending upon any reasoning,

---

*Vol. III, p. 248. Delivered at Madras.

much less on the authority of sages, however great. Thus Vedanta, being based upon universal principles , can alone be the universal religion and not any of those drawing their authority from personalities.

Vedanta recognises the Sages and Incarnations of All Religions

Our sages have however recognised that the vast majority of mankind require a personality. So we have got in our religion provision for a Personal God. And better than having any imaginary idea of a Personal God, we have in this world now and then, living and walking in our midst, the living-Gods, the sages and the incarnations. That leaves the door open for the Hindu to accept the incarnations of all countries in the world. The religion of Vedanta is inclusive enough to take in all the ideals of religions that exist and are likely to come in future.

Besides the incarnations, there are great personages of a secondary character known as the Rishis. A Rishi is the seer of spiritual truths. The nature of the ultimate truths like the existence of God, the soul, the eternal life etc., cannot be understood by exploring the external Nature. It is to be sought only from within. Man in India found out that the soul is not limited by senses nor even by consciouness. Consciousness is only an aspect of Being. Those who have gone beyond the senses and the limited consciousness and have come face to face with the spiritual truths, are the Rishis. "Religion is not in books, nor in theories, nor in dogmas, nor in talking, not even in reasoning. It is Being and Becoming; and till each one of you has become a Rishi and come face to face with spiritual facts, religious life has not begun for you. Till the Super-consciousness is open for you, religion is a mere talk. It is nothing but a preparation.

Not belief in doctrines, nor going to thousands of temples, nor bathing in all the rivers of the world, but becoming a Rishi, the Mantra Drashta or seer of spiritual truths—that is freedom, that is salvation."

Incarnation: Rama and Krishna

Coming to incarnations, the Bhagavata Purana says that there are an unlimited number of them. The chief among them that are worshipped in India today are Rama and Krishna. Valmiki has presented Rama in his work of unmatched literary beauty, the Ramayana as "the embodiment of truth, of morality, the ideal son, the ideal husband, the ideal father and, above all, the ideal king." And then there is Sita, the spouse of Rama, who has been the ideal of Indian womanhood and who will continue to be so in future also.

Another incarnation worshipped in various forms is Krishna, of whom the author of the Bhagavata says, "The other incarnations were but parts of the Lord. He, Krishna, was the Lord Himself." He was the most wonderful Sannyasin and the most wonderful householder in one. He was the embodiment of his own teachings in the Gita—the most conspicuous illustration of non-attachment. Though the most powerful man of his times, he gave up the throne. Than the Gita there is no better commentary on the Vedas. There is no attempted text-torturing in it as in the writings of the commentators. He accepts all forms of worship as steps that gradually lead man to the Absolute Being. The various religious practices like ritualism, image worship etc., are the outcome of the necessity of the human soul. They all gradually lead to that highest ideal of human perfection—the performance of all work without attachment, as an offering to the Divine.

Greater than the ideal of Krishna as the teacher of the

Gita is Krishna the *Gopi-jana-vallabha,* the beloved of the Gopis. There are modern reformers who shun this aspect of Krishna's life as immoral. To them must be said that before they study this aspect of Krishna's life, their minds should be purified of sexuality and greed for gold. "Who can understand the throes of the love of the Gopis?—the very ideal of love, love that wants nothing, love that does not care for heaven, love that does not care for anything in this world or the world to come." In this love of the Gopis, is resolved the conflict between the Personal and the Impersonal ideas of God. The theory of Personal God and the existence of evil is a problem that the intellect cannot solve. Its solution can be found only in what you read about the love of the Gopis. "They hated every adjective as applied to Krishna. They did not care to know that he was the Lord of creation. They did not care to know that he was almighty. They did not care to know that he was omnipotent and so forth. The only thing that they understood was that he was infinite love." Thus, just as in the Gita, Krishna is the teacher of work without attachment, he, as the darling of the Gopis, is the preacher of love for love's sake.

The Buddha

In later times, there developed a conflict between the two powerful communities of India, the kings and the priests. "And from the topmost crust of the wave that deluged India for nearly a thousand years we see another glorious figure, and that was our Gautama the Sakyamuni.....We worship him as God-incarnate—the greatest, the boldest preacher of morality that the world ever saw, the greatest Karma Yogi. As a disciple of himself, as it were, the same Krishna came to show how to make theories practical." Buddha stood for the highest ideal of renunciation. He stood for the poor and the

downcast.   He preached in the language of the people in place
of Sanskrit. But in the course of the expansion of his religion,
it absorbed into its fold, many different barbarous races of
mankind, and all their superstitions and degrading practices
got mixed up with Buddhism, and gradually the religion of
the country came to be dominated by, "the most hideous
ceremonies, the most horrible, the most obscene books that
human hands ever wrote or the human brain ever conceived,
the most bestial forms that ever passed under the name of religion."All this was the creation of the degraded Buddhism.

Sankara and Ramanuja

India had to be lifted from this state of degradation and
that task fell upon the marvellous boy-sage Sankaracharya.
All the hideous races like Tartars and Baluchis had come to
India and become Buddhists. They became assimilated with
us, bringing into our society all their national customs.   "The
whole of our national life became a huge page of the most
horrible and most bestial customs....From that time to
this, the whole work in India is a reconquest of this Buddhistic
degradation by the Vedanta. It is going on and is not yet
finished. Sankara came, the great philosopher, and showed
that the real essence of Buddhism and that of the Vedanta are
not very different, but that the disciples, not understanding
the master correctly, had degraded themselves. They denied
the existence of the soul and of God, and have become
atheists." The Buddhists then began to come back to the
old religion but many of their customs continued to vitiate
the society. Next came the great Ramanuja, who had a great
heart, who felt for the downtrodden and sympathised with
them. He instituted new ceremonies and new methods of
worship. At the same time he opened the door of the highest
spiritual worship to all including the lowest strata of society.

This work spread to the north and found expression through
Chaitanya, the great apostle of Bhakti. Chaitanya represented the mad love of the Gopis. Though himself of the highest
status and a great scholar, he abandoned all this and took to
the life of asceticism and intense devotion. He drew into
his circle people from every strata of society including
Mohammedans. Thus his movement was one of wonderful
liberalism.

Sri Ramakrishna, the Fulfilment of the Line of Indian Sages

Now we come to the modern times. There arose the
need for one who had the large heart of these Vaishnava
teachers combined with the intellect of Sankara; one who
would see in every sect the same spirit working, the same
God; one who would see God in every being; one whose
heart would weep for the poor, for the weak, for the outcast,
for the downtrodden; and at the same time whose brilliant
intellect would conceive noble thoughts that harmonised
all conflicting sects and bring into being a marvellous harmony,
a universal religion of head and heart. Such a sage was born
in Bhagavan Sri Ramakrishna Paramahamsa. He is the
fulfilment of the line of Indian sages, the sage for the time,
one whose teachings are now the most beneficial. His life
and teachings have already attracted large numbers of people
in the East and the West, and in times to come are bound
to attract still larger numbers.

REPLY TO THE ADDRESS AT CALCUTTA*

About Work in the West

Citizens of the capital of this empire! Before you I stand not as a Sannyasin, no, not even as a preacher, but I stand before you as the same Calcutta boy, and talk to you as I used to do. I therefore offer my heart-felt thanks for the unique word that you have used—brother.

The Parliament of Religions was a great affair, no doubt, but my mission in America was not to the Parliament of Religions, but to the great people of America. The Parliament is only an opening, an opportunity. The American nation is a warm-hearted, hospitable people, among whom the feeling of brotherhood has developed more than anywhere else. Their kindness to me is past all narration. So also are our thanks to the English people. No one ever landed on English soil with more hatred in his heart for a race as I did for the English. But as I lived among them and found where the heart-beat of the nation was, I came to love them. I now understand that the difficulties that arise between us and the English people are due to ignorance. To the Western mind spirituality and morality are mainly connected with worldly prosperity. Where they find poverty, they conclude that there is no morality even. But in India the opposite is the case. "Here and here alone is the only race, among whom poverty does not mean crime, poverty does not mean sin .. but poverty has been deified, and the beggar's garb is the garb of the highest in the land. So also all Western manners and customs which seem unseemly to us, have all their meanings if we have the patience to study them."

---

*Vol. III, p. 309

My work in England was more satisfactory to me than my work in America.   The Englishman may be more conservative and not given to express his feelings.   But he is immensely practical and energetic, and once an idea is taken in by him, it sprouts up and immediately bears fruit.   He has a heroic superstructure, and behind this covering of the fighter there is a deep spring of feeling in the English heart.   If you could tap it, he will open his heart, he will be a friend for ever. Therefore, I think that my work in England has been more satisfactory than anywhere else.

Significance of Sri Ramakrishna

You have touched a very deep chord in my heart when you mentioned the name of my Master, Sri Ramakrishna Paramahamsa.   If I have achieved anything by thought, word or deed, it is all due to him.   Only whatever mistakes I have done, are mine.   We read of many prophets in the history of the world.   "Through thousands of years of chiselling and modelling, the lives of these great prophets of yore have come down to us, and yet in my opinion not one stands so high in brilliance as that life which I saw with my own eyes, in whose shadow I have lived, at whose feet I have learnt everything."   A boy born of poor parents in an out of the way village is literally being worshipped even in lands that have looked down on us as heathens.   For, of the power which is manifested here as Sri Ramakrishna Pramahamsa — you have just seen only the very beginnings of its working. It has come for the regeneration of India.   All work in India, social, economic, and political, must come through religion. So religion has been the theme and the rest only the variations in the national life music.   This national ideal of ours is in danger, and the power that is Ramakrishna has come to rectify it and save us from national danger.   The highes

idea in our scriptures is the Impersonal, while the vast majority
of men require a personal ideal, and no nation can arise, or
can become great, without enthusiastically coming under the
banner of one of these great ideals in life. Such a spiritual
ideal has been given to us in the person of Sri Ramakrishna
Paramahamsa and "if this nation wants to rise, take my word
for it, it will have to rally enthusiastically round this
name."

Spiritual Expansion of India

"From this, the idea expands. India must conquer the
world and nothing less than that is my ideal." You have to
expand or perish. This is the law of life. For the past two
generations, India has remained aloof from the world at large,
narrowed herself and shut herself in a shell. This has been
one of the causes of our misery and downfall. This narrow
wall of exclusiveness began to break from the time of Raja
Rammohan Roy. We shall not remain for all time as beggars,
as those who approach for gifts. There must be equal exchange,
if you are to stand on a common level with the others. And
India has got something very precious which the world at
large wants very much—the great spiritual ideals that are
enshrined in her scriptures. The world is waiting for that
treasure; little do you know how much of hunger and thirst
that is outside of India for these wonderful treasures of our
forefathers. "Therefore you must go out and exchange our
spirituality for anything they have to give us; for the marvels
of the region of the Spirit we will exchange the marvels of the
region of matter." To do this we require bands of young
men with will and enthusiasm. "So arise and awake.
The world is calling upon you.... Think not that you are poor,
that you have no friends. Aye, whoever saw money making
the man. It is man that always makes the money. The

whole world has been made by the energy of man, by the power of enthusiasm, by the power of faith."

What we want is Shraddha, which is exemplified in the instance of Nachiketa in Kathopanishad—Nachiketa who dared to go to the realm of death even, for the solution of his problems. Unfortunately Shraddha has vanished from India and that is why we are in the present state. The Western nations have become great because they believe in their muscles, and if you believe in the spirit how much more will it work? "Believe in that infinite soul, that infinite power which your books and sages preach, that Atman which nothing can destroy. In it is infinite power; it is only waiting to be called out......Give up the awful disease that is creeping into our national blood—the idea of ridiculing everything, that loss of seriousness. Give that up. Be strong and have this Shraddha, and everything else is bound to follow....Be not afraid of anything. The moment you fear, you are nobody. It is fear that is the cause of misery in the world. It is fear that is the greatest of all superstitions, and it is fearlessness that brings heaven in a moment. Therefore arise, awake and stop not till the goal is reached."

THE VEDANTA IN ALL ITS PHASES*

Hindu Scriptures and their Characteristics

The Upanishads or the Vedanta, which means the philosophy of the Veda, has silently exercised a great influence on the thought of the world in the past. In India too it is the source of all modern sects of Hinduism like that of the dualists, qualified monists, the Advaitists and all others. Though thus the Upanishads have penetrated through the life of India, there is yet a necessity of preaching it in this country. For though all the sects of India owe allegiance to the Upani-shads, these sects often involve many contradictions, resulting in sectarian disputations. So it is a need of the times to have a better interpretation of the Upanishads, setting forth their underlying harmony. The life of Sri Ramakrishna, at whose feet I had the good fortune to sit, was a living commentary on the text of Upanishads, setting forth their harmony. "It has been my mission in life to show that the Vedantic schools are not contradictory, that they all necessitate each other, all fulfil each other, and one, as it were, is a stepping stone to the other, until the goal, the Advaita, the *Tat Tvam Asi*, is reached." The Veda consists of many more materials than the Upanishads. These parts called the Karma Kanda have now gone out of practice except in so far as traces of it are left in the Pauranika and Tantrik religious practices that are current today. As such, better than calling us Vaidikas, it is proper to call us Vedantists. "The people who call themselves Hindus had better be called Vedantists."

Though there are several sects at present in India with some small differences among themselves, they can all be

---

brought under two main heads—the dualists and non-dualists
Ramanuja is the leading dualistic philosopher of later Indi
and all other dualistic sects have followed him directly o
indrectly in the substance of their teaching and in the organisa
tion of their sects. There have been several non-dualisti
sects also, differing from Sankara, mainly in not acceptin;
the Maya-Vada which they consider as taken from the Budd
hists. But Sankara is the main pillar of non-dualism o
Advaita.

Both Ramanuja and Sankara laid no claim to originality
Ramanuja clearly expressed his position in the very beginnin;
of his commentary on Vyasa' Sutras, stating that he is only
presenting a condensed version of Bodhayana's commentar;
on the Sutras. Sankaracharya also must have more or les:
followed the same method, though he does not state it expressly
anywhere. His Guru and Guru's Guru were in some respect:
more thorough-going Advaitins.

All the other systems of Indian philosophy called Dar-
sanas are also based on the Upanishadic authority. But they
failed to get that hold on India which Vyasa's formulation of
the Upanishadic thought in his Sutras got. Vyasa's system in
itself is in many respects a development of Sankhya philosophy
originated by Kapila. Kapila's psychology and a good deal
of philosophy have been accepted by all the sects of India
with but very little differences. But in spite of all that, it is
Vyasa's Sutras that got a firmer hold than any other in India.
Vyasa himself does not care to reason. His attempt in the
Sutras is only to bring together and, with one thread, make a
garland of the flowers of Vedantic thought. Thus the author-
rity of his Sutras is next only to that of the Upanishads.
Everyone who wants to form a sect in India has therefore
got to write a commentary on Vyasa's Sutras. Next in
authority is the Bhagavad Gita. It goes to the credit of

ankaracharya that he brought it to prominence and wrote
ie most beautiful commentary upon it. Every orthodox
:ct in India has thereafter its own commentary on the
ita.

In later times, many sectarian Upanishads have been
ritten. As Vedic Sanskrit is not very much ruled by grammar,
is easy for one to produce works in that archaic form. But
ese Upanishads, supposed to be 108, and many more by
hers, are not to be taken seriously. Only those commented
on by the great thinkers like Sankara and Ramanuja
serve consideration.

There is one great feature of the Upanishadic thought.
is the most sublime poetry in the world. In the Samhitas, the
ges try to solve the problem of life by letting their mind go
itwards through the senses and they try to paint the Infinite in
rms of external greatness. But they could not arrive at
e secret of life by that method. In modern times, the
esterner also has tried to solve the problem of life by a
idy of external Nature and has failed to get an answer from
ll, dead matter. But while the Western mind has got
anded there, the great thinkers of the Upanishads found
it that an answer to the deep problems of life can only be
t by going inwards. And so we get the Upanishadic
itements like, "From whence the words come back rebound-
g together with the mind," "There the eye cannot go, nor can
e speech" etc. They fell back on the shining soul of man,
id there the answer is found.

In the Atman they found the solution, in the greatest of
Atmans or God, the Lord of this universe—and in His
lation to the Atman of man and man's duty to Him, and
rough that our relation to each other. They described
this in the most sublime poetry in the world. No more
the attempt to paint this Atman in the language of matter.

On the other hand, the description takes the shape o
sublime poetry. "There the sun cannot shine, nor the moon
nor the stars; there this flash of lightning cannot illumine
what to speak of mortal fire."

Impersonality of the Upanishads

The second point that has to be remembered about th
Upanishads is that they are perfectly impersonal. Th
names of many persons are mentioned in it but they ai
simply figures with their shadows moving in the backgrounc
They have no integral connection in the effulgent text of th
Upanishads, which set forth principles. These teachings ai
not against any acceptance of personalities, but they in then
self do not derive their authority from any personality.
Christian missionary once claimed that his scriptures have
historical character and are therefore true. I replied th
mine have no historical character, and therefore they are tru
Your scriptures being historical, they are evidently man-mad
and so non-historicity is in my favour. Man-made texts v
too have. They are the Puranas, the Tantras, the Smrit
etc. The so-called scriptures of other religions are not real
scriptures but only Puranas. For, they also, just like o
Puranas, speak of dynasties of kings, lives of personaliti
occurrences like floods etc.

Some Common points of Agreement Among
Vedantic Schools

Now regarding the teachings of the Upanishads, there a
some which are perfectly dualistic while others are monist
But there are certain points which are common to all sects
India in their understanding of the Upanishads. First the
is the doctrine of Samsara and reincarnation of the soul.
Next they agree in their psychology—first there is the boc

behind that the subtle body constituted of mind and intellect, and behind that even, the Jiva or the living soul. They also agree in holding that the Jiva or the Jivatman, as it is called, is eternal, without beginning but is going from birth to birth until he gets final release. Next there is the most vital point of agreement, that all perfection is in the Atman; the imperfections of living entities arise from the bodies through which it is manifested. Through repeated births, as they get better and better bodies, the perfection of the Atman gets more and more manifested. This is illustrated by an example of a reservoir of water. Through a small hole in its bank only a little quantity of water comes out, but as the hole is increased in size, huge qualities of water begin to flow with great force.

The next point which all the sects of India believe in, is God. The dualists believe in a Personal God in the sense that He is Saguna, possessed of all auspicious qualities and that He is the Ruler, Creator, Preserver and Destroyer of the universe. The Advaitins, however, go a little further, and describe God as Personal-Impersonal. They hold that no adjectives are competent to describe Him. They only describe Him as Sat-Chit-Ananda. The Upanishads go even further, and say that nothing can be predicated of Him except 'Neti, Neti', 'not this, not this.'

What is Purity of Food?

In speaking of the soul as the repository of all power and virtue, and of body being only the field of its manifestation, we come to the question—what is the place of food in regard to that field, the body-mind. There is a famous Upanishadic verse about how with the purity of *Ahara* (food), the purity of *Sattva* (body) take place. Sattva is one of the three constituents of *Prakriti*—Sattva, Rajas and Tamas—, and bodies are constituted of these. In that sense Sattva indicates the body. If the food taken is absolutely pure, the body becomes full of Sattva or capacity for manifesting the glory of the soul. Food becomes impure, that is, not conducive to the development of Sattva, in three ways— one, the quality or the inherent nature of the food stuff, two, the character of the person preparing and serving it, and three, contact with impure things like hair, dirt etc. This is the interpretation of *Ahara-suddhi*, purity of food, which Ramanuja gives, and all the modern exaggerated notions about the purity of food in India have arisen out of this doctrine. But common sense as well experience tells us that a rogue fed on mere milk and rice continues to be a rogue, and cows and deer fed on mere grass continue to be the same animals of their species. Ahara has, however, got a higher meaning, as Sankara interprets it. It means thoughts collected in the mind. When that becomes pure, the Sattva too becomes pure. The solution to this question, therefore, is that purity in both these respects is necessary. But the exaggerated notions of purity of food entertained by people of modern India are absurd.

Dualists and Non-dualists—a Contrast

According to the dualists, the individual souls remain as individuals throughout and God creates the universe out of pre-existing material only as the efficient cause. According to the Advaitists, on the other hand, God is both the material and the efficient cause of the universe. Accordingly Sankara's Advaitic doctrine maintains that God is both the material and the efficient cause through Maya, but not in reality. "God has not become the universe, but the universe is not, and God is. This is the highest point to understand in the Advaita Vedanta, the principle of Maya....This is the challenge—that this world, is a delusion, that it is all Maya, that whether you eat with your fingers or dine on a golden plate, whether you live in palaces and are one of the mightiest of monarchs or are the poorest of beggars, death is the one common end for all. Nations are springing up again and again, and trying to disprove this by becoming great, with enjoyment as their watch-word and power in their hands. They use their power to the utmost, enjoy to the utmost, and the next moment they die. "We stand for ever, because we see that everything is Maya. The children of Maya live for ever, but the children of enjoyment die."

Renunciation, the Chief Condition for Growth of Spirituality

We must guard ourselves against Hegelianism and its baneful influence. Hegel's one idea was that the Absolute is only chaos and that the individualised form is the greater and more desirable. In one word it makes Samsara greater than salvation, and the more you plunge into Samsara, and the more your soul is covered with the workings of life, the better you are for the same. On the other hand our philosophers have from the very first declared that every manifestation, what you call evolution, is a vain attempt of the unmanifested to manifest itself. When this is recognised, the soul of man beats a retreat to the place from where it has come. This is Vairagya or renunciation, and all true religion is based upon it. It is a conviction of all Indian philosophers that without renunciation there cannot be any true religion or morality. Through renunciation alone is immortality attained. It is the power that cares not even for the universe—the power before which the whole universe becomes like "a hollow made by a cow's foot." The spirit of renunciation alone can stand as a warning to a great race against succumbing to the effeminate luxury creeping into India and tending to

make the whole race a race of hypocrites. Though there
may be many in this country whose brains have become
turned by the Western ideals of a luxurious life, I am sure that
there will be thousands in this motherland of mine to whom
religion will ever be a reality and who will ever be ready to
give up without counting the cost.

Another unique idea of the Hindu scriptures is that
religion is to be realised. It is not something that could be
gained through scholarship and study of scriptures. It
comes from the teacher having realisation, to the disciple.
The idea of a family teacher prevalent in Bengal or Kula
Guru system (hereditary Guruship) is an absurdity. A real
Guru is described as *śrotriya* or one who knows the secret
of the Sruti, *avrajina* or sinless, and *akamahata*, or desireless.
Without following this ideal, people call themselves orthodox.
But this orthodoxy is only following certain customs that
came into practice in the days of decadencee. "Go back,
go back to the old days, when there was strength and vitality.
Be strong once more, drink deep of this fountain of yore, and
that is the only condition of life in India."

The Truth about Individuality

According to Advaitists, the individuality that we have
now is a delusion. The Advaitist says that there never has
been an individuality, as constant change is in the nature of
things. It cannot certainly be in the body or mind or thought,
all of which are subject to constant change. Beyond them
is the Atman, says the Advaitist, and this Atman is
Brahman Itself. Take up finite things and go on analysing
them, but you find rest nowhere until you reach the ultimate
or Infinite, and that Infinite, says the Advaitist, is what alone
exists. As against this, people say, 'If I am Brahman, why
cannot I do this and that?' but this is misrepresenting the

position. Your present 'I', the individuality, has to go, and so long as you think of yourself as the limited self, no more are you Brahman.

The dualists however disclaim these ideas of Advaitism, and fight has been going on between them as to which view is true. For the reconciliation of these positions you have to come to Sri Ramakrishna. "It is his life that explains that both these are necessary, that they are like the geocentric and heliocentric theories in astronomy. When a child is taught astronomy, he is taught the geocentric view first, but when he comes to finer points of astronomy, the heliocentric is necessary......Dualism is the natural idea of the senses. As long as we are bound by the senses, we are bound to see a God who is only Personal and nothing but Personal. We are bound to see the world as it is. Says Ramanuja: "So long as you think you are a body, a mind, a Jiva, every act of perception will give you the three—the soul and nature and something as causing both". But yet at the same time when the idea of body disappears, when mind itself becomes finer and finer till it has almost disappeared, when all the different things that make us fear, make us meek and bind us down to body-life have disappeared, then and then alone can one find out the Truth, the grand old teaching—the doctrine of the unity of all existence.

ADRESS OF WELCOME AT ALMORA*

Significance of the Himalayas

It is the hope of my life to end my days somewhere here in the Himalayas, this father of mountains, where Rishis live, where philosophy was born. The Himalayas stand for renunciation, the grand lesson we shall ever teach to humanity. Just as our ancestors used to be attracted by these mountains in the latter days of their lives, so strong souls from all quarters of the earth in times to come will be attracted to this father of the mountains. When all this fight between sects and all those differences and dogmas will not be remembered any more, then mankind will understand there is but one eternal religion, and that is the perception of the Divine within, and the rest is mere froth. These mountains are associated with the best memories of our race. If these Himalayas are taken away from the history of religious India, there will be very little left behind.

THE COMMON BASES OF HINDUISM*

Spirituality as the Heart of India

Before trying to find out the common ground of our national life, we must first of all understand that there is something like a national individuality, just as there is an individuality in every man. Just as every man has got a peculiar line of development set out by his own past Karma, so each nation has a destiny to fulfil and a message to deliver. To have a grasp of this national purpose is the very essence of any vigorous national life. The survival of a nation depends on its faithfulness to its national ideal. There are stories current in which it is said that a certain snake cannot be killed unless the jewel on its crest is destroyed. There are others which say that a certain giant has the soul resting in a small bird on the branch of a tree, and so long as that bird is not killed the giant cannot be destroyed. This is true with nations also. There is a point on which the life of a nation centres, and until that is touched or corrupted, that nation cannot die.

In the light of this analysis we can understand why the Hindus have still survived as a nation in spite of numerous calamities and foreign invasions in the past. Our ancestors in the past, finding that the quest for the secret of Nature through external investigation is useless, turned their attention inward. They focused their attention on this inward quest which is grander, infinitely higher, infinitely more blissful, till it has become the national characteristic, till it has become our second nature. Thus the name of religion and Hindu have become one. This is our national characteristic, the

---

*Vol. III, p. 367. Delivered at Lahore.

source of vitality of the race, and so long as we hold on to this grandest of all of our inheritances, namely spirituality, no external force can destroy us. Bearing this in mind we shall be in a better position to understand why for our national welfare, we must seek out all the spiritual forces of the race. National union in India must be a gathering up of its scattered spiritual forces—a union of those whose hearts beat to the same spiritual tune.

Agreement Among the Various Sects of India

There are many sects in this country. It is the necessity of human nature to have sects; for men think differently. But there need not, for this reason, be sectarian quarrels, because our most ancient books, the Vedas, declare, "That which exists is one; sages call Him by various names." There are certain principles which are common to all the sects that call themselves Hindu. Of these, the first is that we believe the Vedas to be the eternal teachings of the secrets of religion. We believe that this holy literature is without a beginning and without an end, coeval with Nature and the last court of appeal in all our spiritual differences.

The second point of common agreement is that we all believe in God, the creating and the preserving power of the whole universe, into whom it periodically returns, to come out at other periods and manifest this wonderful phenomenon. We may differ in our conceptions of Him, one believing Him to be entirely Personal, another believing Him to be Personal but not human, and yet another holding Him to be entirely Impersonal. All can get support for their positions in the Vedas. One idea may be better than another, but none is bad. Everyone is free to believe and preach his conception of Him.

The third point on which we all agree is the theory of Samsara and the eternity of souls. Nature and man were not

created at any point of time.   There is a cyclic movement of
time and of the universe with it.   For a certain period of time,
the gross material universe is in manifestation and then it
dissolves into its primeval elemental nature to come out again
after an equally long period of abeyance.   Man is involved
in this cyclic process, living and dying and again getting a new
body, until he evolves into his highest possibility and is released
from the cyclic process of Samsara.   He is not only a gross
material body, not only even the finer body constituted of
mind, but basically the Atman which has neither a beginning
nor an end, and knows not what death is.   There will be
differences in the conception of the soul as in that of God,
but we are all one in the basic belief that the soul was never
created, that it will never die and that it will evolve passing
through various bodies till it attains perfection through the
human form.

Divinity of the Soul

Another common point for all Hindu sects—a point in
which we differ from the Western religions—is the acceptance
of the idea that the soul in its essential nature is spirit, pure
and perfect, infinite and blissful.   The dualists may believe
that its powers are contracted in bondage, and monists that
ignorance has made the soul forget its Divinity.   We therefore
close our eyes and look inward when we try to find   God
whereas in other religions they look outwards for their God.
We   must lay   emphasis in our daily life on this idea
of divinity   within and not indulge in self-depreciation,
thinking about our apparent weaknesses.   This faith in
oneself made us great at one time and its loss has brought us
to degradation.   Losing faith in oneself means losing faith
in God.   "I may be a little bubble of water and you may be a
mountain-high wave, never mind.   The infinite ocean is the

background of me as well as of you. I am already joined, from my very birth, from the very fact of my existence, with that infinite life and infinite goodness and infinite power, as you are, mountain-high though you may be."

Another idea special to the Hindu is that religion in India means realisation, and nothing short of that. Mere believing in certain theories and doctrines will not help you much without Anubhuti or Realisation. The greatest proof for the existence of God and of the Atman is not that our reason sanctions it, but because these verities have been seen and realised by the ancients as well as the moderns. There have been thousands of men of such realisation in India in the past, there are still many who have realised, and there will be thousands in the future who would realise.

The Conditions for India's Regeneration

This recognition of your Hindu heritage should make you strong and loving towards all. "Mark me, then and then alone you are a Hindu, when the very name sends through you a galvanic shock of strength. Then and then alone you are a Hindu, when the distress of any one bearing that name comes to your heart and makes you feel as if your own son were in distress."

There is no regeneration for India until you are spiritual. Not only so but upon it depends the welfare of the whole world. Nation after nation has risen and based its greatness upon materialism, declaring man is all matter. All such civilizations as have been based upon such sandy foundations as material comfort, and all of them have disappeared from the face of the world, one after another after short periods of life. But the civilization of India lives even in the present day and there are signs of its revival. Its life is like that of the Phoenix, a thousand times destroyed, but ready to spring up again more glorious. But a materialistic civilisation once dashed down can never come up again.

"Religion for a long time has come to be static in India. What we want to do is to make it dynamic. I want it to be brought into the life of everybody. Religion has, as it has been in the past, to enter the palaces of kings as well as the homes of the poorest peasants of the land. Religion, the common inheritance, the universal birthright of the race must be brought to everybody. Religions in India must be made as free and as easy of access as God's air. And this is the kind of work we have to bring about in India, but not by getting up little sects and fighting on points of difference. Let us preach where we all agree and live with differences, leaving them to remedy themselves."

THE RELIGION WE ARE BORN IN*

Veda the Scripture of the Hindus

Regarding the common grounds of all Hindus, the first point to consider is the scripture. Every religion that has survived and is followed by large numbers of people has one or more scriptures as their support. The Hindu religion is based on the scripture called the Veda, the oldest known scriptural text in the world. The attempts of the Western scholars to fix its date look ridiculous because of the constant change they make even up to the limit of several thousand years in their estimates. The Indian tradition looks upon the Veda as a composition by no man but as "the accumulated mass of endless Divine Wisdom which is sometimes manifested and which at other times remains unmanifested." The Rishis to whom they are attributed are only the discoverers of its truth and nott heir originators. According to Vatsyayana, a Rishi is one who has attained through proper means the direct realisation of Dharma. Even if he be a Mleccha by birth, he is a Rishi. That state is open to anyone even today. The Veda is open to all Hindus for study *Yathemāiṁ Vācaṁ Kalyāṇīmāvadāni janebhyaḥ; Brahma-rājanyābhāṁ śūdrāya cāryāya ca svāya cāraṇāya.* (Sukla Yajur Veda).

The Vedas are divided into two sections—Karma Kanda and Jnana Kanda. The Karma Kanda, taking the form of rituals and fire sacrifices, has now fallen into disuse except to the extent that some of its Mantras and practices survive in the modern ritualistic codes and practices. The Jnana Kanda of the Vedas comprises the Upanishads known by the name of Vedanta, the principles of the Veda. All the Acharyas

---

*Vol. III, p. 454. Delivered at Dacca

quote from the Upanishads and the Vedanta now is the religion of the Hindus. All the sects of Hinduism owe allegiance to the Upanishads, and some of the later cults, where they find it difficult to find sanction in the accepted Upanishads, seek authority in some of the later and unauthentic compositions like Gopala Tapini Upanishad.

There are also other scriptures for the Hindus like the Puranas and Tantras. They are authoritative only to the extent they agree with the Vedas and not otherwise.

The Common Principles of our Religion

Now regarding the principles of our religion, though there are controversies and differences existing among various sects, there are several grounds of unity also. First of all, all of them admit the existence of three entities—Isvara, Atman, and the Jagat or the universe. Isvara is He who is eternally creating, preserving and destroying the whole universe. Then there is the doctrine of the Atman and the reincarnation of the soul. To this is allied the doctrine of Samsara which maintains that innumerable individual souls are taking body after body again and again, and going round and round the wheel of birth and death according to their respective Karmas. Then there is the theory of the Jagat—this universe of movement—without a beginning and an end, but having successive periods of manifestation and subsidence.

The Hindus from time immemorial knew the Atman or the soul to be separate from the mind as it is from the body. So they have the conviction that this embodied state of the Atman leading to repeated births and deaths, with its attendant small joys and great miseries, is not worth having, and it is to be got over through spiritual disciplines. The attainment of this goal is Moksha or liberation.

Most of the Hindu sects accept the Avatara Vada, which

attempts to see God through Man, instead of going to God through Nature.

Next, there is image worship. It is accepted by all Hindu sects in spite of all the denunciations of it as idolatry by the reformers. Next, regarding the deities who are worshipped, there are the five Devatas who are to be worshipped in every auspicious rite. All the other Devatas are merely the names of certain states held by them, and even these five Deities are nothing but the different names of the one God. In spite of the many imperfections that have found entrance into the image worship as in vogue now, the practice as such does not deserve condemnation. "Ah! Where would I have been if I had not been blessed with the dust of the holy feet of that orthodox image-worshipping Brahmana!"

REPLY TO THE MADRAS ADDRESS*

Realisation as the Test of Religious Truth

Your appreciation of my humble work in the cause of the religion and spiritual ideals of India shows that in spite of the downfall and degradation that our country has undergone, the spiritual foundation upon which our culture rests is still sound and stands unshaken, strong as ever. The evolution of spiritual humanity is the mission that India has been fulfilling among the races of the world.

The one idea that Hindu religion holds forth before its followers is that man must realise God, even in this life. Thus to realise God, Brahman, as Dualists would say, or to become Brahman, as the Advaitins will say, is the aim and end of the whole teaching of the Vedas, and every other teaching therein contained, represents a stage in the course of our progress thereto. Just as the Absolute Brahman is true, so are relative truths—all the different sects, standing upon different manifestations of the same Brahman, as realised by illumined ones in India or elsewhere, are also true. Only some are higher than others. Suppose a man starts straight towards the sun. At every step of his journey, he will see newer and newer visions of the sun, until he reaches the sun itself. All these views of the sun, each view progressively larger as it is closer to the sun, are really of the sun and are therefore true. But none of them can claim to be exclusively true. Similarly all the various religions and sects are true— some nearer, some farther off from that Infinite and Absolute Being, the one without a second. "The Vedas are the only scriptures which teach this real Absolute God, of which all

*Vol. IV. p. 277.

other ideas of God are but minimised and limited visions. As the Sruti takes the devotee gently by the hand, and leads him from one stage to another, through all the stages that are necessary for him to travel to reach the Absolute, and as all other religions represent one or other of these stages in an unprogressive and crystallised form, all the other religions of the world are included in the nameless, limitless, eternal Vedic religion."

Deathless India

There are several reform societies who, with a superficial outlook, attribute all the evils found in presnet day Hindu society to religion. Their attempt at reforming life in India by destroying its religion is as misconceived and ridiculous as the man in the story wanting to kill the mosquito that sat on his friend's forehead by dealing such a heavy blow as would have killed the man. But their efforts have failed and are bound to fail because their idea of reform is to go against the evolution of India for the past several millenniums, in short to kill India and make it into an imitation Europe. "And will she die? This old mother of all that is noble or moral or spiritual; this land which the sages trod; the land in which God-like men still live and breathe? I will borrow the lantern of the Athenian sage, and follow you, my brother, through the cities and villages, plains and forests, of the broad world—show me such men in other lands if you can! A tree is known by its fruits. Go under every mango tree in India and pick up bushels of the worm-eatern, unripe, fallen ones from the ground, and write hundreds of the most learned volumes on each of them. Still you have not described a single mango. Pluck a lucious, full-grown, juicy one from the tree, and now you have known all that the mango is. Similarly these man-gods show what the Hindu religion is. They show the character, the power and the possibilities of that racial tree which counts culture by centuries, and has borne the buffets of a thousand years of hurricane, and still stands with the unimpaired vigour of eternal youth."

The World Needs Indian Thought

Those reformers who hold contrary views should observe the quaint phenomena accruing to religion in the West. Under the onset of modern scientific research, all the old forts of Western dogmatic religions are crumbling into dust, and Western theology is at its wit's end to accommodate itself to this ever-rising tide of aggressive modern thought. While in such a situation man in the West is drifting away from church and religion, it is only the religion which has drunk the water of life at that fountain of light, the Veda, namely, Hinduism and Buddhism, alone are reviving. The restless Western athiest or agnostic finds in the Gita or in the Dhammapada the only place where his soul can anchor. The tables have thus been turned, and the Hindu now finds that only his religion can stand the test of modern scientific criticism and enquiry, and that others are attempting to re-state their religion after the Hindu plan. He finds that he has neither to torture texts nor commit any other form of intellectual dishonesty to save his religion. Nay, he may call all that is weak in his Scripture, weak, because they were meant to be so by the ancient sages, to help the weak, under the theory of Arundhatinyaya.

Divinity of the Spirit in Man

"Let us take our stand on the one central truth in our religion—the common heritage of the Hindus, the Buddhists, the Jains—the spirit in man, the Atman of man, the immortal, birthless, all-pervading eternal Soul of man, whose glories

the Vedas cannot themselves express, before whose majesty
the universe with its galaxy upon galaxy of suns and stars
and nebulae is a drop. Every man or woman, nay, from the
highest Devas to the worm that crawls under your feet,
is such a spirit evolved or involved. The difference is not in
kind but only in degree. The infinite form of the Spirit,
brought to bear upon matter, evolves material development;
made to act upon thought, evolves intellectuality; and made
to act upon itself, makes of man a God.

"......Manifest the Divinity within you, and everything
will be harmoniously arranged around it. Remember the
illustration of Indra and Virochana in the Vedas. Both were
taught their divinity but the Asura Virochana took his body
for his God. Indra, being a Deva, understood that the
Atman was meant. You are the children of Indra, you
are the descendants of Devas. Matter can never be your
God; body can never be your God.

"India will be raised—not with the power of the flesh,
but with the power of the Spirit, not with the flag of destruction
but with the flag of peace and love—the garb of the Sannyasin;
not by the power of wealth but by the power of the begging
bowl.. Sitting in luxurious homes, surrounded with all the
comforts of life, and doling out a little amature religion may
be good for other lands, but India has a truer instinct. It
intuitively detects the masks. You must give up. Be
great. No great work can be done without sacrifice. Even
the Purusha sacrificed himself to create the world. Lay
down your comforts, your pleasures, your name, fame or
positions, nay, even your lives, and make a bridge of human
chains over which millions will cross the ocean of life....
Ours is to work. The results will take care of themselves.
If any social institution stands in your way of becoming
God, it will give way before the power of the Spirit. I do

not see into the future, nor do I care to see. But one vision I
see clear as life before me: that the ancient Mother has
awakened once more, sitting on Her throne, rejuvenated,more
glorious than ever. Proclaim Her to all the world with
the voice of peace and benediction."

CAUSES OF INDIA'S DOWNFALL AND
WAYS OF RECONSTRUCTION*

1. *Isolation from world community:* "No individual or nation can live by holding itself apart from the community of others, and whenever such an attempt has been made under false ideas of greatness, policy or holiness—the result has always been disastrous to the secluding one. To my mind, the most important cause of the downfall and the degeneration of India was the building of a wall of custom, whose foundation was hatred of others round the nation, and the real aim of which was to prevent the Hindu from coming into contact with the surrounding Buddhistic nations ...."

"Give and take is the law, and if India wants to raise herself once more, it is absolutely necessary that she brings out her treasures and throws them broadcast among the nations of the earth, and in return be ready to receive what others have to give her. Expansion is life, contraction is death. Love is life and hatred is death...."

"We must therefore mix with all the races of the earth. And every Hindu who goes out to travel in foreign parts renders more benefit to his country than hundreds of men who are bundles of superstitions and selfishness, and whose one aim in life seems to be like the dog in the manger. The wonderful structure of national life which the Western nations have raised, are supported by the strong pillars of character and until we can produce numbers of such men, it is useless to fret and fume against this or that power.

---

*Vol. IV, p. 365. Summary of Ideas from Reply to the Calcutta Address.

2. *Pseudo-renunciation:* We sometimes talk foolishly against material civilisation. Now there may be about a hundred thousand really spiritual men in India. But should several hundred million men be sunk in savagery and starvation for the sake of the spiritualisation of this small number? How was it possible for the Mohammedans to conquer the Hindus? It was due to the Hindus' ignorance of material civilisation. If India is to be raised, the poor are to be fed and educated, and priestcraft and social tyranny must be removed. If you root out priestcraft from Hinduism, you get the best religion. Everybody must have equal opportunity and you get the best religion. "Can you make a European society with India's religion? I believe it is possible and must be."

3. *The abandonment of the original idea of Jati:* "The original idea of Jati was the freedom of the individual to express his nature, his Prakriti, his Jati, his caste, and so it remained for a thousand years." This means the freedom of the individual to grow according to his natural endowment, his inherent qualities. Only by allowing this process will a species throw out variations, but with the stopping of variations decay and death will gradually step in. It was this that happened to India when the original idea of Jati was given up and in its place was created compartmentalised endogamous groups called castes. Any crystallised custom or privilege or hereditary class in any shape really prevents Jati from having its full sway, and when any nation ceases to produce this immense variety, it must die. . . . Every frozen aristocracy or privileged class is a blow to Jati. Let Jatis have their sway; break down every barrier in the way of caste (real Jati), and we shall rise. Now look at Europe, when it succeeded in giving full scope to Jati and took away most of the barriers that stood in the way of individuals developing their own Jati—Europe rose. In America there is

the best scope for real Jati to develop, and so the people are great. Every Hindu knows that astrologers try to fix the caste of every boy or girl as soon as he or she is born. That is the real caste, the individuality—and Jyotisha recognises that. And we can rise only by giving it full sway again. This variety does not mean any inequality, nor any special privilege."

The Hindus have to give up nothing, but only to move on in the line laid down by the sages and shake off their inertia, the result of centuries of servitude. During the several centuries of Muslim domination, all progress was lost and the Hindu social institutions have remained in the incomplete form. Now the building has to be completed— not on the lines suggested by renegades and foreign missionaries, but along our own lines. Each nation has a main current of life. In India it is religion. Make it strong, and then everything will be set right.

MY LIFE AND MISSION*

India Decadent, Not Dead

India looks today like a big dilapidated building, and at first sight one will feel that there is no hope for India. But a nation will not be destroyed until the essential principle, for which it has stood through the ages, is destroyed. It is just like a man not ceasing to function even if his coat has been stolen away twenty times, because the coat is unessential. India has been invaded by several races, and it has been despoiled of its wealth. But the soul of India has not yet been seriously affected. Its soul consists in religion. There will be no more India if the people change their religion and their institutions, because that is the vitality of that race. It will simply disappear.

"In spite of poverty and loss of freedom, India is holding fast to the idea that the real is God and everything else is but His shadow. She clings to this like grim death." So India is still living, and like a patient who keeps up his vitality amidst a crippling illness, she has still hopes of a resurrection from her present state of downfall and degradation.

The uplift of India has to be attempted through vitalising her religious life which forms the soul of the nation. But there is no reason why India should necessarily be poverty-stricken. An ascetic ideal should not be imposed for the benefit of a few sages. That would be 'the tyranny of the sages.' This has to change. While the spiritual pursuit continues, the material condition must improve. Along with spiritual administration, steps have to be taken for improving the material condition of life as well.

---

*Vol. VIII, p. 73.

Regeneration Through Sannyasa

In India this has to be done through religion, as religion is the one thing they understand. My idea is therefore to press the Sannyasin Orders of India into this work. I myself belong to one of these monastic Orders. My Master was a great saint and a man of the utmost renunciation. By practising all religions, he discovered that all religions lead to the same goal. Along with me there were about a dozen other young men whose lives were revolutionised by contact with him. We became a closely knit brotherhood bound together by mutual love and devotion for a cause. The cause is the spiritual ideals of our Master, mainly the experiential nature of the spiritual verities like God and the Atman, and the truth of all religions being paths to the same goal. But we had to face tremendous difficulties. None took us seriously, and we had to face the ridicule and neglect of men. We were Sannyasins without any financial resources, who got our food by holy alms. We, however, congregated in a dilapidated house as the centre of the Brotherhood, but for a long period of more than ten years we could make no impact.

I wandered all over India from Himalayas to Cape Comorin as an itinerant monk. Not finding sufficient response in India, I came to the States to attend the Parliament of Religions. Some friends now came forward to help me. I was able to raise a little fund and start two papers. Besides lecturing in several parts of the States, I went over to England and worked there.

My plan is to mobilise the large numbers of Sannyasins in India to work for the uplift of the masses. It is only through religion that India will take any idea. The Sannyasin is therefore fit to be a teacher. He commands the respect of the people. They are now only spiritual teachers but they must now be trained also to carry secular knowledge to the masses. It will be very difficult to get pupils into schools, so the teacher has to go to the student.

But the Sannyasins have to be trained for the purpose. For this, with the kind help of some American and English friends I have started two centres, one in the Himalayas and the other at Calcutta, the capital. I want to see that a centre exclusively for women also is started. Once started, men should not have anything to do with it; for, the women's cause has always suffered when men took up the task of shaping the destinies of women. This part of the work has yet to be started. Through My Master's Consort, Sri Sarada Devi, this is to be achieved.

WOMEN OF INDIA*

Woman as Mother

The men and women constituting a nation represent an ideal that is being worked out through them. So to understand a people we must have a grasp of the ideal for which they stand. To judge them by other standards than theirs is not fair or correct. To think of one's own ideal as perfect and criticise others for differing, is not a valid procedure; for, if we carefully observe we will find that all ideals develop certain aberrations in the course of their application to life. A people should not be judged by these aberrations.

The mother is the ideal of Indian womanhood. The word woman calls up the idea of the mother in the Indian mind. And even God is conceived of as Mother. From his childhood the Hindu learns to adore motherhood.

In the West, woman is essentially a wife. In a western home the wife rules, but in an Indian home it is the mother that rules. The wife has to be subordinate to her. In the concept of the mother woman stands above all carnality. Woman as mother is 'marvellous, unselfish, all-suffering, ever forgiving.'

In India it is the father that punishes the child, not the mother as in the West. In a Hindu home, the mother walks in front; the wife follows only. The mother is the mistress of the family; the son's daughter is under her government. A son does not like to see his wife over-riding his mother.

Woman as Wife and Daughter

To be the mother of a child, is a sacred task to the Indian

---

mind. A child must be born in prayer and not in lust. He is an Aryan who is born through prayer, says Manu. A child born otherwise, he considers as illegitimate. This attitude of sanctity with which the Hindu mind regards motherhood, springs from the conviction that it is the pre-natal influences that give the impetus to the child for good or for evil. Education and all the rest are secondary. The mother has to keep her body and mind pure if she were to conceive a noble son. "For, that which brings forth the child is the holiest symbol of God Himself. It is the greatest prayer between man and wife, the prayer that is going to bring into the world a soul fraught with a tremendous power for good or for evil.

. "The worship accorded to the mother has its fountain-head there. She was a saint to bring me into the world. She kept her body pure, her mind pure, her food pure, her cloth pure, her imagination pure, for years, because I would be born. Because she did that, she deserves worship."

Hindu society is socialistic, as the individual has to live for the caste to which he belongs. So marriage is not a mere private affair. The good of the society is dependent on it. So the individuals have not much to do in settling marriages. It is the parents or the caste that settles it. The system of early marriage is also an off-shoot of it. For if the parties have no choice in the matter, it is better that it is settled before they develop preferences.

.Widowhood

Another feature of women's life which looks very anomalous to outsiders is widowhood. In the higher castes of India there is much disproportion between the number of men and women. Women are larger in number, and so there is no chance of every one of them getting married. The institution of widowhood was the way in which the socialistic outlook

of the Indian society tried to mitigate the difficulty. Widowhood withdrew a large number of women from competition
with those who had not even one chance of marriage. "Either
you have a non-marriagable widow problem and misery, or
the non-husband-getting young lady problem." Widowhood
is thus a process of social adjustment. It no doubt caused
hardship to a large number of people. A widow, cultured
and well-instructed, does not consider life a hardship. She
lives a life of asceticism and devotion, thus elevating her
life to higher levels of perfection. Thus while widowhood is a
hardship to many, it is also, a doorway to higher spiritual
perfection to many others.

Daughter in the Family

A daughter in a Hindu family poses a great difficulty to
parents. Marriage opportunities being limited owing to
considerations of caste, a man has to spend beyond his means
to give an attractive dowry to the bridegroom and his parents.
Sometimes families are absolutely impoverished by this.

The civilisation of India stands for the spiritual emancipa-
tion of man. The Hindu mind is deeply imbued with a
sense of the evanescence of all worldly values and
glories. All the races that set great store by such values have
gone to oblivion after a few centuries of vigorous national
life. But Hindu institutions have stood the test of ages. The
Hindus have lived through the ages, because they have learnt
that the world is evanescent and that the spirit alone abides.

MODERN INDIA*

Pre-Buddhist Polity in India

In pre-Buddhist India, the power of the priests was based on the faith that the kings and the people in general had in the efficacy of the sacrificial Mantras of the Vedas. The priest had the mastery of these Mantras, and therefore the power derived from it. The sacrificial cult of the Vedas taught that through these Mantras and through the rituals performed with their chanting, the favour of the Devas could be obtained. On the favour of the Devas depended the welfare of the royal dynasties, and also abundance of rain for the prosperity of their kingdoms. Thus though the king was vested with all powers, he was a suppliant at the door of the priest, who regulated their conduct not only in religious matters but even in the affairs of State. Not only that, the kings were aware that it is only if the priests were pleased with the performance of many sacrifices at which they got much wealth as sacrificial gifts, could they hope themselves and their dynasties glorified in the traditional annals like the Puranas which were compositions of the priests.

To carry on the Government, to propitiate the priests, and to live an ostentatious life—the king required wealth. For this he had to drain the resources of the subjects, especially of the Vaisyas, the trading community.

The common people were nowhere in the picture. They had no power over the rulers who governed them, and their voice was not very much felt in shaping the policies of the governments. It is not that germs of self-government were not there in the country. There were several small republics,

---

*Vol. IV, p. 438.

but they were mostly controlled by aristocratic families. In villages there was the rule of the five, the Panchayat, which dealt with all local matters. But these self-governing institutions did not grow enough to exercise control over, and give direction to, the affairs of the State.

Theoretically no external authority was required to control the king. He was controlled by the sacred laws given by the Rishis. Many of these laws were wise and beneficial. But who is to enforce them? If the king was high-minded and had a dedicated sense of his own position, he would adhere to the sacred laws. Otherwise, they were ineffective in controlling him.

Rise of Kingly Power in the Buddhist Age

The polity was gradually revolutionised when Buddhism became a widespread religion and many of the ruling princes became its votaries. This process finally resulted in the formation of the Mauryan Empire ruled by the great Buddhist emperor Ashoka. Under Buddhism the Vedic sacrificial cult and the priests who had mastery of the Veda, had no place. With this the priests lost power, which passed into the hands of emperors who ruled over vast areas bounded by the ocean. This period ended when the empire broke up giving place to many small kingdoms under Rajput princes.

Brahmanical priestly power also once again tried to assert itself, as auxiliary to royal power. From the Vedic time onwards, though the priests largely controlled the kings, there were movements among the latter for asserting their power. This often led also to struggle between the king and the priests, culminating in Buddhist imperialism. It was from this state of affairs that a resurgence of priestly power now took place, not as a rival of royal power but as its ally. But neither the kings nor the priests had the brilliance and

originality of earlier days. The chief task before their combined forces was the extirpation of the common enemy,
Buddhism.   In this process the spoliation of others' properties,
sucking the blood of the masses, and wreaking vengeance on
enemies became their chief occupation.   Besides, among the
royal classes of those times were included many barbarian
tribes coming from outside India,   who were made into
Kshatriyas and other Varnas by obliging Brahmanical priests.
All the corrupt practices of these new entrants also vitiated
the atmosphere of the times.   The combined effect of all this
was that the country became an easy victim to the invasion
of Muslims of Tartaric origin from beyond the frontiers. For
the Muslim invaders the Brahmin priest was of no account.
They were Kafirs, and the most liberal treatment they could
give them was to allow them to spend their lives quietly in
silence till death overtook them.

Muslim Rule and Resurgence of Imperialism

Though the Muslim power was foreign and had no regard
for the Vedic traditions, it was in a way a reassertion of
Imperial power had.   It was in the heydays of Buddhism,
that Imperial Power asserted itself, suppressing the priestly
domination. With the rise of Rajput power, the priestly
power had again begun to reassert.   But any further lease of
life was denied to it by the establishment of Muslim Imperialism.   Being foreigners professing an alien faith, the Muslim
rulers had no use for Brahmanical ritualism just like the
Buddhist emperors.   The grand State rituals like Asvamedha
and Rajasuya, which enriched the priest and reinforced his
power, disappeared altogether from the land.   The priest
had to be content with officiating at a private level.   His
language,Sanskrit,also lost its importance as State language,

that place being taken by Arabic and Persian. In this way for a few centuries Imperial power under the guise of foreign rule re-asserted itself in India to the exclusion of Brahmanical influences.

East India Company and Rise of Merchant Power

At the end of this period of Imperialism took place the advent of a new power that was entirely different in outlook and ideals from all ruling powers of the past. This was the establishment of British power in India, which was a phenomenon entirely new to the people. It was the power of a class of merchants, the East India Company, that established the British Empire in India. The merchant, representing the Vaisya, was in the past a despised community exploited by the priest (Brahmana) and the rulers (Kshatriya). Most of the servants of the Company who came from England were men descended from blue-blooded aristocrats. Before the shrewed intellect and diplomacy of this .merchant power, the empires of Hindu and Muslim dynasties disappeared in spite of the valiant opposition put up by them. This assertion of the merchant or Vaisya power was a phenomenon absolutely novel to India.

India had known the times when the priest, with his superior intelligence, learning and his widely accepted claim to possess power to curse and to control Natural phenomena like rain, dominated the kings and the lives of the people. It had also experienced the despotic rule of Kshatriyas, the fighting class, to whom everyone had to submit like slaves. But now in the domination of the mercantile power represented by the East India Company, the country had a totally novel experience.

The Ages of Dominance of the Priest, the King, the Merchant and the Worker

This phenomenon is a feature of social evolution in human history. The class division of man into Brahmana, Kshatriya, Vaisya and Sudra according to their character type based on the dominance of Sattva, Rajas and Tamas, seems to prevail all over the world and at all times. Human history shows that each of these classes gain ascendency in a succeeding order in all countries. Among all the ancient nations—the Chinese, the Egyptians, Sumerians, the Babylonians, the Chaldeans, the Aryans, the Iranians, the Jews and the Arabs—the Brahmanas or the priests guided the society in the first period of their history. Absolute monarchies and oligarchies representing the Kshatriya wielded power in the next period. Among the modern nations, beginning first with England, the power of controlling society has passed from the priest and the king to the rich mercantile and industrial classes, the Vaisyas.

There were in the ancient world some powers like those of Troy and Carthage which look like merchant power. But these were not really so. They were controlled by the descendants of royalties who had mastery over all the wealth of the land and took to mercantile activities. None else were allowed to be thus engaged. In Egypt, the oldest civilisation, the priestly power prevailed only for a short period, and society became subjected to the royal power. In China, with the help of the institutions of Confucius, the royalty controlled the State till recent times. Lamaism was the last relic of priestly power, but even that came under royal control. In India the dominance of royal power continued even long after the decay of great empires, until the emergence of the East India Company. It is only among the Jews that the priestly power kept the royal power and the Vaisya power away from exercising control over society.

Just as royal power subdued priestly power in ancient times,so in modern times, under a different set of circumstances, the Vaisya power has come to dominate. England is the representative of that power. The power of the wealthy classes is behind all the organisational might and technical advancement of England and other Western nations. The conquest of India is not the conquest of Jesus or the Bible but of England "whose war flag is the factory chimney, whose troops are the merchantmen, whose battle fields are the market places of the world, and whose Empress is the shining Goddess of fortune herself." What new revolutions will be effected under the aegis of this power,cannot be predicted on the basis of India's past, because the experience is entirely novel and discontinuous with the past.

Priestly Power, Its Achievements and Failings

It was stated before that the four classes Brahmana, Kshatriya, Vaisya and Sudra will in succession dominate the world. Now the period of domination of each will have its own characteristic, some beneficial and some adverse. In the priestly domination there is great manifestation of Sattva Guna. Intellectualism and spiritualism are the results of it. The priest, being universally respected, had no difficulty for his livelihood, and could therefore devote his time for literary and intellectual pursuit. The dominance of Sattva Guna in the Brahmanical character, produced many with highly developed psychic capacity, enabling them to penetrate the thick walls of Tamas that separate the sensate from the supra-sensual realms. Thus the priest was the first to discriminate between the body and the spirit and understood their distinctiveness. It was by their intellectualism and spiritual power that the priest could control the ferocious energies of the fighting class. He could impress on the kingly class that his power was of a higher order than the martial power of theirs. He could by the Mantra control Natural phenomena like rain, and, by his power to curse, ruin those who opposed him. The priestly power stood as a moderating influence between the kingly clans and the common men. The common man had no hand in the affairs of the State and was often the subject of oppression and exploitation by the kingly class. The priest tamed and controlled the kingly class and was thus a friend of the common man.

Priestly power has got its undesirable characteristics as well. The priest claimed to have power over the subtle world, which cannot come under the observation of others, as the gross external Nature can. Secrecy and fraudulence gradually enter into the ways of people dealing with subtle forces, especially when the motive of self-aggrandizement begins to dominate their mind. Besides, the mind develops a craze for the smoky world of obscure mysticism, which gradually develops into obscurantism. Ritualism comes to dominate life and enslave the human mind to its rigid framework. Obscurantism and ritualism gradually develop a mentality given to superstition and slavishness that shuns originality and all forward movements in life. Hypocrisy and exclusiveness complete the degeneration of the mind. Priestly exclusiveness seeks to guard all its knowledge a secret for keeping up its ascendency, until those branches of knowledge of which they are the custodians, perish for want of men versed in them. Accumulation and concentration of knowledge and wealth are necessary to make them effective, but at the same time if there is no effort to disseminate them and make them available for the good of all, the consequence is degeneration and utter collapse ultimately. Wisdom, knowledge, wealth, strength, prowess and whatever else Nature gathers and provides us with, are only for diffusion when the moment of need is at hand. We often forget this fact, put the stamp of 'mine only' upon the entrusted deposits and *pari passu* sow the seed of our own disaster.

The collapse of priestly power becomes complete when for the sake of greater gain, members of that class begin to take to other professions like service and business.

Kingly Power—Its Achievements and Failings

The decline of priestly power is followed by the rise of kingly power. The king is like a lion. The lion kills animals ordinarily, but not the fox that is subservient to it. Royalty wants enjoyments, and so it encourages fine arts, architecture and other means for the enrichment of life. The craze for power leads them on to a career of conquest and formation of big kingdoms and empires. As an aid to this, military power is developed to the maximum extent. The king always stands for the concentration of power in himself. To make his power absolute, the docrine of the Divine Right of Kings is developed. The king becomes a representative of God, and the sanction of his power is interpreted as coming, not from any human source but from God himself. Kingship then gradually develops into tyranny. If the people concerned are a virile set, they rise in revolt and bring the king to book. But if they are weak and docile, they submit like slaves. The result is the utter degeneration of the king as well as the people, and the country becomes an open field for invaders.

Merchant Power—Its Achievements and Failings

The priest or the Brahmana represents learning. The

king or the Kshatriya represents the sword. When both
these sources of power fail, a new power gains domination.
That is money power, represented by the Vaisyas. When the
Vaisya power reaches its maturity, it is able to guard itself
from being swindled by the superior intelligence of the Brahmana or robbed by the physical power of the Kshatriya.
His freedom to charge exorbitant interest gives a whip in the
hands of the Vaisya to control the others. The power of
money enables him to control the others.

The Vaisya becomes a great missionary of culture. For
the sake of trade the merchant has to travel to distant lands,
and he carries with him the wisdom and the arts and the
sciences acquired during the time of the dominance of the
other classes. For the acquisition of wealth he also develops
industries and the production of various goods, and thus
promotes the growth of capital. But the Vaisya too is selfish
like the other two classes, and seeks by hook or by crook to
concentrate all power and wealth in his hands. None of these
three classes can really pass on wealth and power to the Sudra,
the masses, by the sweat of whose brow the Brahmana,
the Kshatriya and the Vaisya are enabled to gain pre-eminence
and prosperity during their period of domination. The
Sudra or the mass-man is the basic foundation of every
society. Even if he is kept away from power, the other
classes have to keep their contact with him if they are to keep
up their vitality. One of the reasons for the gradual decay of
these classes is the lack of mass contact.

At the present time the Vaisya, is represented by the British at the meridian of power. The English nation is essentially
a nation of traders. By money power he has mastered the
means of production and controls the reins of government.
It is no wonder that the conquest of India on behalf of Britain
was accomplished by a business firm, the East India Company,

which represented that country. Such a phenomenon the
world had never witnessed before in its history.

Total Degradation of India to Sudrahood

This conquest has been accomplished at a time when
India's national life was at its lowest ebb, with the failure of
the priestly and the royal classes to hold the country together
owing to the degradation that had come over them, resulting
from their alienation from the masses, the Sudras. "Let
alone her Sudra class—her Brahmanas, to whom belonged
the acquisition of scriptural knowledge, are now the foreign
professors; her Kshatriyas, the ruling English men; and her
Vaisyas, too, the English in whose bone and marrow is the
instinct of trading, so that only the 'Sudraness'—the status
of being the beasts of burden—is now left with the Indians
themselves. A cloud of impenetrable darkness has at present
equally enveloped us all. Now there is neither firmness of
purpose nor boldness of enterprise, neither courage of heart
nor strength of mind, neither aversion to maltreatments by
others nor dislike of slavery, neither love in the heart nor
hope nor manliness. What we have now in India are only a
deep-rooted envy and strong antipathy against one another;
a morbid desire to ruin by hook or by crook the weak; and a
dog-like tendency to lick the feet of the strong. Now the
highest satisfaction consists in the display of wealth and
power, devotion in self-gratification, wisdom in the accumulation of transitory objects, Yoga in hideous diabolical practices,
work in the slavery of others, and civilisation in a base imitation of foreign nations, eloquence in the use of abusive
language and the merit of literature in extravagant flatteries
of the rich or in the diffusion of ghastly obscenities!" In
this state of decadence all the classes of India have, as it
were, been reduced to the state of the Sudra.

Rise of Sudra Power in the Future

In different parts of the world the Sudras have always been held in suppression in spite of their numerical superiority, because they could not unite. But changes are coming among the Sudras. In Europe the people were reduced to Sudrahood by the Roman aristocracy, but Europe today is filled with Kshatriya valour. In India too under a foreign government the traditional higher castes have no special governmental the patronage. The suppressed and the depressed classes of people are getting better facilities of education, and some improvement is being gradually effected in their condition. But these are only the faint beginnings of the new age. The upliftment that they have received is only through absorption of some of the characteristics of the Vaisyas and the Kshatriyas. "But a time will come when there will be the rising of the Sudra class, *with their Sudrahood*—that is to say, not like that at present, when the Sudras are becoming great by acquiring the characteristic qualities of the Vaisya or Kshatriya—but when the Sudras of every country, with their in-born Sudra nature and habits, and not by becoming in essence Vaisya or Kshatriya, but remaining as Sudra, will gain absolute supremacy in every society. The first glow of the dawn of this new power has already begun to slowly break upon the Western world, and the thoughtful men are at their wit's end to reflect upon the final issue of this fresh phenomenon—socialism, anarchism, nihilism and such other sects which are the vanguard of the social revolution that is to follow."

Awakening of India

By the friction with her foreign rulers and by the modern system of education introducing the strange ideals of foreign nations, India is slowly awakening from her long and deep slumber. The first stage of this awakening is characterised by the tendency to imitate everything coming from the West and to evalute India's own ideals and ways of life by applying the standards derived from the West. The West stands for individual independence, for money-making education and for dominance of politics in the life of the people. India through the ages has stood forMukti as the goal of life and for renunciation of worldly values as the means for it. In this situation we have to remember: "By imitation, other's ideals and ideas never become one's own—nothing, unless earned, is one's own. Does the ass in the lion's skin become the lion?" "On the one side, New India is saying: 'What the Western nations do must surely be good; otherwise how did they become so great?' On the other side, old India is saying: 'The flash of lightning is intensely bright, but only for a moment. Look out, it is dazzling your eyes. Beware!' "

While India has to learn many things from the West, it should not be by imitation, but by thoughtful absorption. For this Indians must first of all be conscious about the worth of the essential values of their own culture. So: "O India! with this mere echoing of others, this slavish weakness, this vile detestable cruelty, wouldst thou, with these provisions only, scale the highest pinnacle of civilisation and greatness? Wouldst thou attain, by means of thy disgraceful cowardice, that freedom deserved only by the brave and the heroic! Oh India! Forget not—that the ideal of thy womanhood is Sita, Savitri, Damayanti; forget not—that the God thou worshippest is the great Ascetic of ascetics, the all-renouncing Sankara the Lord of Uma; forget not—that thy marriage, thy wealth, thy life are not for sense pleasures,are not for thy individual personal happiness; forget not—that thou art born as a sacrifice to the Mother's altar; forget not—that thy social order is

but the reflex of the Infinite Universal Motherhood; forget not
—that the lower classes, the ignorant, the poor, the illiterate,
the cobbler, the sweeper, are thy flesh and blood, thy brothers.
Thou brave one, be bold, take courage, be proud that thou
art an Indian, and proudly proclaim: I am an Indian, every
Indian is my brother. Say—the ignorant Indian, the poor and
destitute Indian, the Brahmin Indian, the Pariah Indian, is
my brother. Thou too clad with but a rag round thy loins
proudly proclaim at the top of thy voice: 'The Indian is my
brother, the Indian is my life, India's gods and goddesses
are my God, India's society is the cradle of my infancy, the
pleasure-garden of my youth, the sacred heaven, the Varanasi
of my old age.' Say brother: 'This soil of India is my highest
heaven, the good of India is my good', and repeat and pray
day and night: 'O Thou Lord of Gauri, O Thou Mother of the
Universe, vouchsafe manliness unto me, O Thou Mother of
strength, take away my weakness: take away my unmanliness,
and make me a Man!' "

THE EAST AND THE WEST*

The Misconceived Picture of the Cultures

The Indian and the Westerner see the superficial aspects of each other's life, country and culture and form one-sided view of the central, life-giving ideal behind the civilisation of each other. In India the Westerner sees abject poverty, malnutrition, famished condition of men and animals, dirt accumulated everywhere, hovels amidst palatial buildings, visitations of plague, cholera, malaria and famine, and every possible sign of degradation and decay. They find on the body of India a population of three hundred million men swarming like so many worms on a rotten, stinking carcase. These men are uneducated, ill-clad and half-starved. While patient and long-suffering in their down-trodden and abject condition, they are none the less malicious, cunning, given to jealousy and sneaky like slaves. Divided into numerous castes, the stronger ones indulge in violence and oppression against the weak, while behaving with abject submissiveness to their foreign master. They find in Indian religion a bundle of superstitions, encouraging heinous practices like idolatry, untouchability, infanticide, widow-burning etc. Something like this is the estimate of India and the Indian by a superficial Western observer.

Indians also see their foreign masters in similar lurid colours. They find in them a race of people maddened by the wine of power; fierce like wild beasts, hen-pecked, lustful and drenched in liquor; eating every kind of forbidden meat; mixing freely with women and dancing with them held in

*Vol. V, p. 441.

each other's arms; addicted to self-aggrandisement and exploitation of others; holding the body to be the Atman; having no faith in the hereafter; and maintaining an outlook wholly absorbed in the senses and the pursuit of creature comforts.

The National Ideal

Both these are superficial views, without penetrating deep into the people's life and grasping what it is that keeps it functioning. Every nation has a national ideal which it has been specialising in, and which is at the same time essential for the life of the whole world. A nation lives so long as it is still true to this national ideal pertaining to it and is thus capable of contributing something for the life of the world. The moment a nation becomes incapable of representing its national ideal and thus ceases to be of use to the world as a whole, it perishes, giving place to new people. That India is still alive today, in spite of the fact that it has passed through vicissitudes capable of totally wiping out a people, and has thus been carrying on an existence through several millenniums is proof that it is still alive and remaining true to its national ideal and retaining its capacity to contribute its share for the good of the nations of the world.

There are a set of people calling themselves reformers, who go about criticising and condemning everything Indian, and declaring that we are a week and hopeless people, and cry hoarse to the Westerner to help us in our sad plight. They also do their best to imitate the Westerner in all respects, believing that it is the way of uplifting the nation. They are totally mistaken in their understanding of India and its culture. Indian culture and religion have made their impact in the past in countries far and wide in the south-east up to

Indonesia and Australia, in the north-east up to Tibet, China and Japan, and in the north up to Siberia.

Besides, these cultural ideals of India still prevail here vigorously. "Here in India will ever be the old Siva taboring on His Damaru, the Mother Kali worshipped with animal sacrifice, and the lovable Sri Krishna playing on His flute. Firm as the Himalayas they are; and no attempt of any one, Christian or other missionaries, will ever be able to remove them."

Dharma and Moksha Ideals

Let it be understood that good qualities are not the privileged monopoly of any one nation only. There can of course be greater prevalence of one ideal of character in one nation than another. With us the prominent idea is Mukti (liberation); with the Westerners, it is Dharma....Here the word Dharma is used in the sense of the Mimamsa-sastra. What is Dharma? Dharma is that which makes man seek happiness in this world and the next. Dharma is established on work. Dharma is impelling man day and night to run after, and work for, happiness.

"And what is Mukti? It is what teaches that even happiness in life is slavery, and that the same is with happiness in life to come, because neither this world nor the next is beyond the laws of Nature....Again happiness, wherever it may be, being within the laws of Nature, is subject to death and will not last *ad infinitum*. Therefore man must aspire to become Mukta; he must go beyond the bondage of the body; slavery will not do. This way of Moksha prevails only in India and nowhere else. Hence is true the oft-repeated saying that Mukta souls are only in India and in no other country."

There was a time in India when these ideals of Dharma

and Moksha were cultivated side by side. We find in the Mahabharata such votaries of Dharma like Yudhishthira, Arjuna, Duryodhana, Bhishma and Karna functioning side by side with aspirants of Moksha like Vyasa, Suka, Janaka etc. But the harmony between these two ideals ceased during the days of Buddhist ascendancy. Buddhism and Jainism were monastic religions, and especially in Buddhism every man was encouraged to take to monasticism without much consideration of his fitness for it. This was a great mistake. Education, habits, customs, laws and rules should be different for different men and nations, in conformity with their difference of temperament. To declare to the householders that Moksha alone is worth while in life is a blunder. The law for him is the pursuit of Svadharma—the pursuit of one's duty accruing to one according to one's nature and station in life. The householder has to earn money by fair means. He has to do his duty in life. He has to care for his family. For him to passively submit to wrongs done by others, is a sin. He has to do good works, as far as is possible for him. "If you cannot do that, how do you profess to be a man? You are not a householder even—what then to speak of Moksha for you!" Moksha may be a superior ideal, but you become fit for its pursuit only after going through the school of Svadharma.

It has been said that Dharma is based on work. The nature of Dharma is constant performance of action with efficiency. Men are repeating Mantras and practising meditation, but no qualitative improvement is found in them. This is because their minds have not yet attained that strength and refinement for the effective practice of these disciplines of Moksha. To use the technical language of Vedanta, they do not possess that Chitta-suddhi, or mental efficiency, which only dedicated performance of Svadharma can generate.

Freedom from the Tyranny of the Moksha Ideal

It will be objected that works are mixed with some element of evil. In spite of this defect, to work is better than doing no work. By abstaining from work, a man who is not fit for a meditative life will only fall into Tamas or inertia—become lifeless, passive, dull as dead matter. This state of Tamas is the very opposite of Sattva, the quality conducive to spirituality and characterised by calmness, illumination and transcendence of pleasure and pain. It is about such Sattvikas or men endowed with mental purity that the Lord says, "He who has no enemy and is friendly and compassionate to all, who is free from the feelings of 'me and mine' even-minded in pleasure and pain and ever forbearing." But to the man who is not a Sattvika the Lord gives exhortation to work for prosperity. To them he has said: "Yield not to unmanliness, O Partha. It does not befit thee. Abandon this faint-heartedness and arise for action." The Indian people have not heeded to this exhortation of the Lord for the past several generations and all their troubles stem from this negligence.

The Balanced Outlook of Vedic Religion

The Vedic religion has got in it place for all the four great values of life—Dharma, Artha, Kama and Moksha. Under the influence of Buddhism and Jainism an undue stress was laid on Moksha to the exclusion of the other values—"Either you must have Moksha or you are doomed to destruction." These are the only two ways held forth by them, and there is no middle course. This attitude was an injustice to the ordinary man, for whom work and enjoyment are very necessary for growth. It led to degeneracy, causing the replacement of Sattva-guna by Tamo-guna, the quality of dullness and ignorance, in the national mind. It is only the Vedic religion that works for the all-round development of man, which leads him gradually through the secular values to Moksha. In the post-Buddhist India, the reformers like Kumarila and Sankara tried to revive the Vedic ideal of four-fold Purusharthas (values of life) and this practice of Sva-dharma—the discharge of duties that accrue to one according to one's nature and aptitude. But India is a vast country with teeming millions inhabiting it. The work of regenerating them cannot be done in one day.

Hinduism a Living Entity

It has been said that each nation has a national purpose and character of its own. The French, for example, have equality and national independence as their characteristic trait, and in the English character, the 'give and take' policy, the business mentality of the trader, is dominant. They would not stand taxation, unless they know why it is required and how it is spent. As far as the Hindus are concerned, they say that "political and social independence are well and good, but the real thing is spiritual independence—Mukti." In point of Mukti all Hindu sects alike accept it. The Hindus will stand any trials and tribulations, so long as their aspiration for Mukti is not affected. In spite of all the tragedies through which our nation has passed none of these traumatic experiences have been able to destroy this firm-rooted national ideal. It is just like the story of a giant who could not be killed, however much you might injure him; because his heart, the centre of life principle, is located in a bird in a nearby tree. So until that bird is killed the giant also cannot be killed. Such is the case with India. That she is still a living entity, is because her spiritual ideal, the quest after Moksha or spiritual freedom,for which she has lived through the ages, remains still intact.

Now there are people who question the use of keeping up this national ideal any longer. They think, it is better to convert this Indian nation into a race of materialists. Now taking for granted that such an attempt is in the right direction,the question can be asked whether such a course is possible. The Hindu national character is the result of the evolution of several millenniums,and to turn it backward is as impossible as to divert the course of the Ganga to its source. Just as any attempt to do so will mean the dissipation and drying up of the water of the stream, any attempt to rub off India's past entirely and begin anew, will mean the death of the nation.

It is, however, sheer ignorance and want of proper understanding that makes people think that our national ideal has been an unsound and mistaken one. It has kept us alive and is keeping us so in spite of all the degeneration we find round about. If a person wants to make an intelligent comparative study of the life and manners of other nations with ours, then let him first read our scriptures and travel all over India mixing intimately with all strata of society. It will then be clear as noonday to him that the nation is still living intact and that its life is surely pulsating. You will find then also that hidden under the ashes of apparent death, the fire of our national life is yet smouldering and that the life of this nation is religion, its language religion, and its ideal religion: and your political work, social reform, plague-prevention work, famine relief work—all these things will have to be done, as they have been done all along here, only through religion. Otherwise all your frantic yelling and bewailing will end in nothing.

Do not be dazzled by the political system of the West,

and do not imitate them under the impression that their ways form a panacea for all our ills. In spite of all the show of freedom of vote and grandiose political institutions, it is the few rich that control the Governments there, and the tribe of politicians "rob others and fatten themselves by sucking the life-blood of the masses in all European countries". Behind the screen these politicians indulge in a "revelry of bribery and robbery in broad daylight". The rich control Governments, and besides robbing the people, send them as soldiers to fight and be slain on foreign shores, so that in case of victory, their own coffers may be full of gold bought by the blood of the subject people shed on the field of battle.

It is not therefore correct to imitate them under the misguided impression that they are all good and that we have nothing of worth in our ideals and institutions. While guarding ourselves against their mistake, we have to be aware of the fact that we have many things to learn from other nations. The nation which thinks that it has nothing to learn from others is on the brink of disintegration. A nation with vitality will always keep itself open to outside influences and learn valuable lessons from whatever sources they may come, but will absorb and express those lessons in its own way, and not imitate the ways of others.

Who are the Aryans

Man, according to us, has three different aspects—body, mind and soul. Let us first take up the physical aspect of life in studying the contrast between the East and the West. First there is the question of colour and race. Variety in complexion is due to mixture of blood. Climate can influence it, but not radically. For, there are white aborigines in tropical regions like Borneo and Celebes and the colour of the Eskimos of the North Polar regions and the aborigines of Canda is not white.

"According to the Hindu Sastra, the three Varnas of Brahmana, Kshatriya, Vaisya, and several nations outside India, to wit, the Cheen, Hun, Darad, Pahlava, Yavana and Khash were all Aryans." The Cheen was not the present Chinaman, but a powerful nation living in north-eastern part of Kashmir. The Darads lived in the hills between India and Afghanistan. Huns ruled in the north-western parts of India. The Yavanas were the Greeks. The Khash were the semi-civilised Aryan tribes living in the Himalayan hills. They may probably be the ancestors of modern Europeans.

Modern scholars hold that the Aryans had reddish-white complexion, black or red hair, straight nose, and well-drawn eyes. Wherever this has changed, it is due to race mixture. They hold that at present there are only some tribes on the west of the Himalayas who are of pure Aryan blood.

All these are only speculations of scholars. "Let the Pandits fight among themselves. It is the Hindus who have all along called themselves the Aryans. Whether of pure or mixed blood, the Hindus are Aryans; there it rests. If the Europeans do not like us, Aryans, because we are dark, let them take another name for themselves—what is that to us?" Whether white or dark, the Hindus are the handsomest people in the world. In point of health, we are inferior to the Westerners. This is largely due to the deficiency in our diet and our poverty, and above all by the custom of early marriage. The Westerner is a meat-eater and his diseases are mostly of the heart and the lungs. The Indian is a vegetarian and his ailments are mostly of the stomach.

Progressiveness

The loose Indian dress, especially the Sari, is artistic,

but the Western dress is tight and more suited for work than the Indian dress. The Indian has specialised in making golden ornaments for beautification, and the Westerner in dress making. Paris is the centre that sets the fashion of women's dress, and London, of men. Men and women of high society in America all order their dress from these foreign countries in spite of the very high costs because of heavy import duties.

"This world, if you have got the eyes to see, is yours—if not, it is mine. Do you think that anyone waits for another?" The West is very vigilant in studying the world round about, and making innovations from stereotyped ways of life, in order to promote material advancement. But the Indian sticks to the Sastras and persists in moving in the old grooves insted of moving with the times and developing originality. The consequence is poverty and backwardness.

Cleanliness and Elegance

There is great difference in the practice of personal cleanliness between the Indian and the Westerner. A bath of the whole body, preferably a plunge-bath, is a must for the Indian. In the West such body bath is not considered essential.* A bath once a week is considered sufficient, and then they change only their inner clothing. There may be some justification for it in the cold regions of Europe, but it is so even in warm regions like Italy and Spain. Washing of exposed regions like head and hands are considered bath. Even in high-style hotels in fashionable Paris, baths are not to be found. If one wants a bath, one has to go to a public bath, paying five rupees.

(*Here it must be rememberd that Swamiji is speaking of Europe and America of the late 19th Century).

Hindus take body-bath in water for fear of incurring sin otherwise. They do not therefore take much care to rub off oil and dirt. Unlike in the West, as climate is generally warm in many parts of the country, and as clothing is scanty, bathing is an easy operation in India, but not so in the West. Most of the customs and habits of life are necessitated by climate and environment. Rinsing the mouth, bathing etc., can be done publicly in India, but not in the West.

We in India try to practise personal cleanliness but in the process of doing this, we have no hesitation to heap dirt in our premises and outside.

In the West there is an orderliness, elegance and artistic sense in the homes and daily life of people. We too had these qualities in our traditional ways of life. But these are being fast given up, and we are trying to imitate the Western ways in a very imperfect manner. In arts like painting and sculpture we are trying to be mere imitators of the West, and are not therefore able to attain those standards of perfection seen in old Indian art.

On Matters of Food

The Upanishad says that when the food (Ahara) is purified, the inner senses get purified. Ahara means food, but interpreting it according to its root, it means anything that is taken in. All sense perceptions are taken in by us, and so the purity demanded is of the sense impressions we absorb. It is better to understand it in both the senses.

Ramanuja says that food can be defective in three ways: (1) *Jatidosha*: It consists in the inherent nature of certain items like garlic etc., which are supposed to be exciting. (2) *Asrayadosha*: It is the defect arising from the character of the person who handles or gives it. (3) *Nimittadosha*: It consists in pollution by dirty objects like hair While these principles are sound, we in India have misinterpreted and mis-applied them. In the name of Asraya-dosha, we have been practising all forms of 'don't touchism'. All kinds of Lokacharas or local practices are taken as sacred rules, which is absurd. "In these matters, the Acharas or the practices of the Great Acharyas or teachers should be followed. It is better for us to bestow some more attention on Nimitta-dosha, which arises from not following hygienic methods. We observe some external forms of ceremonial purity, but we awfully break all hygienic rules. The bazaar sweets exposed to dust and dirt, and often stale and polluted, are consumed in flagrant violation of the rules of Nimitta-dosha. These sweets and all kinds of fried stuff and highly spiced dishes and fermented food are not only spiritually condem-nable, but are ruinous even from the physical point of view as great health hazards. Diabetes and dyspepsia are the their inevitable consequences in the long run, while infectious diseases like dysentery and cholera form their immediate results.

Next there is the question of meat eating, on which views are sharply divided. The strongest argument against it is that it involves the infliction of pain on, and slaughter of, other living beings. To this it is replied that it is impossible to sustain life without killing some other forms of life. Vegeta-tions too are living beings, and their destruction is also killing. As for infliction of pain, in agricultural and other food pro-ducing processes, heartless cruelty is shown to animals.

The Sastras also differ on the question of meat-eating. While the Buddhists, Jains and the Vaishnavas invariably prohibit slaughter for food, the Hindu Sastras make it com-pulsory on certain occasions. They hold that killing animals except for sacrifice is sinful, and they allow sacrificial meat to be taken. One who does not kill animals and offer meat

to the guests is condemned. Manu says that those who do
not take meat at Sraddha and certain other ceremonies will
be born as animals for such refusal. The modern Vaishnavas
will find it difficult to reconcile themselves to the idea of Rama
and Sita taking meat, as stated in Valmiki's Ramayana.

There are opinions condemning animal food on various
grounds. Some say animal food produces various diseases. As
against this, it is pointed out that if this is true, non-vegetarian
races like the English, Americans etc. must have been the most
unhealthy, and the Hindus the most healthy, people. But this
is not so in fact. Next it is contended that those who eat goats
and swine will have brains like the brains of those animals. To
this it may be replied that on this principle, potato and brinjal
eaters must have potato and brinjal brains. It is argued that all
the chemicals of the animal food are contained in vegetable
food also, and the former is therefore superfluous. As against
this, it can be replied that the elements of these chemicals are
all there in water and sunlight. Why not subsist on them only?

In this way many things are said for and against these
two forms of diet. We have to adopt one view or the other
on the basis of the practical effect seen in the long run. It is
seen that nations that live on animal food are found on the
whole stronger, more courageous, and warlike. They have
overcome the vegetarian races and dominated over them. So
the conclusion is that in a world where there is struggle for
existence, nations and races have to take animal food, if they
are not to be overcome and enslaved by others.

"To eat meat is surely barbarous and vegetable food is
certainly purer. Who can deny that? For him surely is
suited a strict vegetarian diet whose one end is to lead solely
a spiritual life. But he who has to steer the boat of his life
with strenuous labour through the constant life-and-death
struggles and the competition of this world, must of necessity

take meat.   So long as there will be in human society such a thing as the triumph of the strong over the weak, animal food is required, or some other suitable substitute for it has to be discovered; otherwise the weak will naturally be crushed under the feet of the strong.   It will not do to quote solitary instances of the good effect of vegetable food on some particular person or persons.   Compare one nation with another, and draw conclusions.   The judicious view admitted by all in regard to this vexed question is, to take such food as is substantial and nutritious, and at the same time, easily digested.   The food must be such as contains the greatest quantity of nutriment in the smallest volumes, and be at the same time quickly assimilable. Rice, dal, whole-wheat chapati, fish, vegetables and milk can constitute an adequate diet. He who can afford it can take meat also.

Food habits vary from country to country.   But there are some common features.   The poor in all parts of India take mainly cereals of some kind or other according to their availability in a place, along with herbs, vegetables and small quantities of fish and meat according to their means. In the West they take bread and potatoes, small quantities of meat and fish and some kind of wine. The well-to-do people in the West subsist mainly on meat, and cereals form only a subsidiary part. The dinner is the main meal of the day. The rich have French cooks, and their dinner consists of eight courses.   Several of these courses are of fish and meat in different forms.   Each course is served in a different plate with only one item at a time. The plates are changed for each course. With almost every course, a different kind of wine is served.   After the dinner coffee without milk is taken. Primitive man subsisted on game, before he began cultivtion. So the meat obtained by hunt had to be kept for some days, probably dried, and it got somewhat rotten and smelling. So preference for meat somewhat stale and smelling has remained among men in the West.   If it is not meat, some other smelling substance like cheese or garlic is taken. The Jews have peculiar rules of eating like Hindus—for example they do not eat fish that have no scales, nor pork, nor cloven-footed animals; nor meat cooked in the same place where milk and milk preparations are made, or meat which is not offered to God.

In India people generally sit on the floor and eat from metallic plates or leaves kept on the floor. In some parts small desks are placed in front to place the food.   Other prohibitions also exist regarding food. Bengalis do not eat fowl or chicken eggs, but they take duck's eggs. So also the Nepalese. Kashmiris take the eggs of wild duck but not of domesticated ones. Generally all communities that take the meat of goats take also fowl.

Most of these rules and prohibitions about food must have arisen from considerations of health and local conditions. They have been changing in the West and the East, and in modern times most of these old taboos have been abandoned, except where strong religious compulsions persist.

Civilisation in Dress and Manners

The dress of the ancient Aryans was only a Dhoti, and a Chudder. While fighting, the Kshatriyas wore a kind of trousers. In many parts of India a turban is the most essential part of dress. In many Buddhist sculptures, even noble persons are shown with very little dress, but always with a turban.

The dress of the Greeks and the Roman too was Dhoti and Chudder, except when fighting.   It was after Alexander's conquest of Iran that the Greeks learned of more refined forms of dress.   The Iranians must have taken it from the Chinese, who were the primeval teachers of civilisation. The Chinese were using a variety of dresses like coats, caps and trousers.

In hot countries dress, except for covering what is considered improper to expose, was not a necessity. It was more of an embellishment. But in cold countries it was an unavoidable necessity. So from the covering made of animal skin dress evolved into various type of coverings like blankets and shaped dresses like pants, coats and so on. As body had to be covered for protection, many ornaments could not be worn in cold countries. So while ornaments of a variety developed in hot countries for display, refinement of dress took its place in the cold countries.

The fashions in dress, especially for women, is set in Europe by the French, while that of men by the English. All rich people from the countries of Europe and America order their dress from Paris and London. The fashion set by these countries changes very frequently. Conformity in dress to the set standards is enforced in the West by social compulsion. The expensive and fashionable nature of dress is taken as the sign of a man's status in the East and the West.

People of Europe and America are very particular about privacy. Being a hot country we take a lot of water and prefer open air. But people in the West, being meat–eaters and their country being cold, take much less quantities of water, but sip small quantities of wine. Sneezing, belching, and gargling are allowed in public in our country, but not so in the West. But they allow the blowing out of the nose in a pocket hand-kerchief. Rinsing the mouth, spitting, picking the teeth etc. in public are prohibited in polite society. In England and America one has to be very guarded in conversation with women. One should not speak of leg or of indigestion and other stomach complaints. The French, the Germans and the Russians are not so sensitive in these matters.

Conversations on being in love are frequently carried on between parents and sons and daughters, and among them-selves; it is a habit alien to the standards of Indian social behaviour.

Westerners are Shakti worshippers in a realistic sense. Woman is given very great importance. Even in worship it is to Mary that prayers are mostly addressed among the Catholics. '*Ave maria*' is the cry heard everywhere. With the Westerners Shakti Pooja is not ritualistic as ours but actual. In the West the woman's State is foremost, and great personal attention is paid to her. Such special regard is paid not merely to the noble born or young women, but even to a stranger or a mere acquaintance.

France and its Capital Paris

France and its capital Paris constitute the centre of Western civilisation. Paris matures or ripens every idea of Western ethics, manners, and customs, good or evil, that gains currency in the West. The country is picturesque, neither too cold nor too hot, and blessed with an abundance of water, grasslands, charming hills, rivers and springs. Men too are so fond of beauty that they embellish the glorious endowments of Nature with their artistic skill.

The Renaissance movement that came after the discovery of the old Greek civilisation would not have made an impression on Europe, had it not been for the fact that the Franks took it up by the 16th century. The remarkable French character is, as it were, the incarnation of the ancient Greek that had died only to be re-born in the spirit of the French— always joyful and full of enthusiasm, very light and silly yet again exceedingly grim, prompt and resolute to do every works, and again despondent at the least resistance. But that despondency is only for a moment with the Frenchman; his face soon after glows with fresh hope and trust.

The Paris University is the model of European universities and all Academies of science are varitations of the French Academy. In the military art and in the literary art, the French set the standard. Again France is the home of liberty. The French Revolution released the cry of liberty, fraternity and equality, which now echoes at first in all European countries and will eventually echo all over the world.

Often people in India hear only of the darker side of life in Paris. But such dark features are characteristic of all metropolitan cities. The distinctiveness of the French is that they make even sensuous enjoyments so artistic and attractive that people from all the world over, with plenty of money, go there to get the best forms of sensuous enjoyments. Longing for enjoyments is there in all countries. Only the French have learnt to cater to it with a scientific thoroughness in place of the vulgarities of other capitals.

As everywhere chastity of women is given an important place in France also. But the Frenchman is, however, a little freer in this respect, and like the rich men of other countries, cares not for criticism of his laxity. This springs from their having enjoyment as the goal of life. "Each nation has a moral purpose of its own, and the manners and customs of a nation must be judged from the standpoint of that purpose. The Westerners should be seen through their eyes. For us to see them through our eyes, and for them to see us with theirs—both these are mistakes. The purpose of our life is quite the opposite of theirs....Our goal of life is Moksha. How can that be ever attained without Brahmacharya or absolute continence?.. The purpose of life in the West is Bhoga, enjoyment. Hence much attention to strict Brahmacharya is not indispensably necessary with them, as it is with us."

Modern France is the creation of the events that followed

the great French Revolution,which led to the emergence of the
great Napoleon Bonaparte. The Revolution did away with
much of the past tyrannical regime of the kings, which was
symbolised in the prison   called Bastile. Under Napoleon,
France over-ran a greater part of Europe,until he was defeated
at the battle of Waterloo and sent into exile. Among his
successors, it was Napoleon III that created modern Paris.
In order to impress the people, he undertook this scheme, and
to keep them contented by giving them work, he undertook
the task of systematically rebuilding the city, wiping out its
old alleys and lanes, and filling it with well-laids roads and
gardens and beautiful buildings. Thus arose the boulevards
and the fine quarters of d'Antin and other neighbourhoods,
and the avenues of the Champs Elysees, which are unique in
the world.

Social Evolution in the East and the West

The perception of the unity of all existence is the goal of
all knowledge. Unity of all existence is accepted by Western
science also. The name of that One is Brahman. The
perception of separateness is an error. It is called Maya,Avidya
or nescience. How the One has become the many is not
known to Indian spiritual science or to the Western material
science. But the variation of that One, the different sorts
of variation and individualities it is assuming, can be understood, and the enquiry into this is called science. The doctrine
of evolution is the study of how the one primitive form of
life gradually developed into more complex forms. Man too
is not accepted as born in a civilised state all of a sudden. He
evolved from a primitive animal-like condition into the
civilised state. Proofs of the early states of man when he
lived in caves are coming to light, and what is more, there are
men who live in such conditions even now. Originally, using

only flints as instruments, they gradually learnt the art of fusing soft metals like tin and copper to make instruments· The ancient Egyptians, Babylonians and Greeks were at this stage of civilisation for long and did not know the use of iron, though they used gold in abundance.

At first man was a hunter of animals. Later he began to domesticate them, the dog being one of the earliest of such species. Originally a hunter for food, he later learnt agriculture and the way to improve the wild cereals into cultivable and consumable species. Nature is effecting very gradual changes in plants and trees, but man's interest in them as food made him find ways and means to speed up their change.

In the primitive stage there was no marriage. Promiscuity was the order. Next developed matriarchy, according to which wealth was in the hands of women and paternity was unimportant and did not count for inheritance. Polyandry also went together with matriarchy in many societies. At a later stage man asserted himself as the more important factor in society, and consequently patriarchy and the modern marriage system came into vogue.

In the beginning of civilisation society was divided according to the regions people lived in and the occupations they followed. There were people living on the sea-shore and earning a living by fishing; hill men who hunted animals; and nomads of deserts who kept flocks of goats and sheep. The dwellers on the plains developed agriculture and thus became more and more civilised. They began to live in houses and subsist more and more on grains and vegetables, unlike the others who lived mostly in the open, facing Nature's inclemencies and eating meat as diet. The former therefore gradually grew more mild and peaceful, while the latter, the hunter, the shepherds and fishermen, became more hardy and warlike. So when there was scarcity of food, these more

virile people attacked and plundered the more civilised and
mild agriculturists of the plains. For self-protection, the
agriculturists had to come together in large numbers. Thus
small kingdoms developed.

These warlike hillmen can be called the Asuras, and the
mild civilised men of the plains the Devas. The Asuras,
being stronger and more warlike, often defeated and plundered
the Devas of the plains, but the Devas, being more intelligent,
invented machines that could be used against the warlike
Asuras. These conflicts between the Devas and the Asuras
resulted in the formation of well-organised States.

With the development of States, society became more
complex and those representing the different types like the
mountaineers, fishermen, dwellers of the plains etc. had to live
together. But the tendencies that developed from a hoary
past, dividing people into Asuras and Devas, persisted and the
society came to have on the one hand pirates, brigands and
fighters and on the other, mild peasants. Men of different
dispositions, civilised and savage, born with the nature of
Devas and Asuras, have become fused together to form
modern society. The dominance of the Daivi or Asuri
nature determines the nature of a society.

Other kinds of stratification also developed in organised
society. One section of people went on producing wealth
by physical or intellectual labour. This wealth had to be
protected from the depredations of the Asuras. The section
that offered to protect is represented by the king and the
fighting class. There was another section who offered to
purchase the articles of utility from its producers and to
exchange or to sell them among those who wanted them in
the country or in far off places. They were the traders. Then
these classes, the protectors or the kings and the traders, did
little in actual production, but managed to get the lion's share

of the produce or profits of the works of the agriculturists
and others, because of their key position in society.

Rise of Civilisations of Asia and
Europe

The whole of Asiatic civilisations rose in the plains on
the banks of the Ganges, the Indus, the Yangtse-kiang and the
Euphrates. The foundations of these civilisations were laid
by the Devas, the agricultural people living there. The
European civilisations rose on the hills and the sea shore,
from people who began as pirates and robbers. These were
therefore characterised by the Asuric tendencies. Central Asia
and Arabia too seem to have been inhabited by Asuras who
united in hordes after hordes to attack the Devas and then
force them to flee their lands and scatter all over the world.
Large numbers of these people went to Europe and mixed
with the barbarian races there. As a result the civilisations of
Greece and Rome gradually took shape. The Romans brought
under their sway most of Europe, except the northernmost
part of it inhabited by barbarians. But the Romans were
gradually degenerated by wealth and luxury. Their empire
was now over-run and destroyed by the barbarians of
the north, who were forced to expand southwards by the
pressure of Asura races from Asia. By the fusion of these
Asiatic Asuras, the Western barbarians and the remnants
of the Romans and the Greeks, a new race sprang up. The
Jews also had been earlier driven away from their home and
scattered all over Europe. Into this social milieu Christianity
entered. All these hordes of Asuras, these different races and
their creeds and ideas, heated by the fire of constant struggle
and warfare, began to melt and fuse in Mahamaya's crucible;
and from that fusion the modernEuropean people have sprung
up. During this process, the two heads of Christian Churches

the Pope of Rome and the Patriarch of Constantinople gained influence over those brutal barbarian hordes, over their kings and queens.

Rise of Islam and the Crusades

In another region of the world, among the wild nomads of Arabia, arose another religious movement, which became a great world force. It was the rise of Islam. Under the banner of Islam the wild Arabs over-ran all the countries about them, Persia, Asia Minor, Afghanistan—all lands upto India, which they could not penetrate—besides the whole of North African coast and even Spain in Europe. By the time the Arab waves of expansion had subsided, the central Asian Asuras known as Seljuk Turks embraced Islam, and they extended the work of Islamic expansion started by the Arabs. It is these Turks and Tartars that little by little overran the whole of Northern India, and became one with the people there by intermixture with the Hindus and the people of Persian origin. In the process their flat round faces changed and they developed the appearance of a new type of people. These Tartars and Turks were purely Asuric in temperament. They never cared for learning like the Arabs. The only thing they understood was fighting, and wherever their blood has been mixed, mongrel fighting races have come into being.

The Tartars seized also the throne of the Arabian Caliphs. They took possession of Jerusalem and other sacred places of the Christians. The heads of the Christian churches grew mad with fanatical rage at them and they exhorted the kings and the nobles under them to recover these holy places. As a result Crusades came to be organised by the kings and nobility of all Europe against the heathen Turks. Armies marched from Europe to these distant places only to perish at the hands of inclement climate and the Turkish warriors. But

one good came out of this movement. It brought the barbarous people of Europe into contact with the culture of
India and Greece, which the Arabs had taken to their empire,
now under the occupation of Turks. This resulted in the
organisation of an Order of Monks called the Knight Templars,
who took up a philosophy akin to Advaitism and held up
Christian dogmas to ridicule. They were eventually suppressed by the fanatical Catholic Church.

A tribe of Arab Muslims called the Moors, spreading
through the African coast, invaded Spain and established a
Moorish kingdom there. During their supremacy the learning that the Arabs had gathered from the Greeks reached
Europe in the dark ages, when Christian Europe was
under the domination of the Catholic Church, which stood
against the spread of learning among men in general. Unlike
the Catholic Europe of Medieval times, Islam encouraged
learning. They founded the first universities of Europe, and
students flocked to them from all parts of Europe. The
sons of nobility went there to learn polished manners, etiquette
and the arts of peace and war.

Europe also learnt a new military organisation from the
Moors. When Muslim armies conquered a country, the
ruler divided the land between his generals and noblemen.
They got all civil and administrative powers, and in return
they were to provide the king with a fixed number of soldiers
and be always ready to take up arms on his behalf. Thus the
kings organised armies without much expenditure for themselves. When the system was adopted in Europe, one important modification was introduced in it. Among the Muslims
the king and the feudatory chiefs left the ordinary citizens to
live their own lives. But in Europe every one had to live
under the protection of a feudatory chief and be ready to

work in his estates and fight when he wanted. Thus the
vast majority of subject people were turned into serfs.

Progressive Civilisation—the Western and the Eastern

The so-called progressive civilisation of the Europeans
involves successful accomplishment of the desired object even
by wrong means, i.e. by making the end justify the means.
It makes acts of theft, falsehood and hanging appear proper
under certain circumstances. It guides and justifies the well-
known European ethics which says, "Get out from this place.
I want to come in and possess it." The truth of this is borne
out by the evidence of history, that wherever the Europeans
have gone, there has followed the extinction of the aboriginal
races.

"The European civilisation may be likened to a piece of
cloth of which these are the materials: its loom is the vast
temperate hilly country on the seashore; its cotton is a strong
warlike mongrel race formed by the intermixture of various
races; its warp is warfare in defence of one's self and one's
religion. The one who wields the sword is great, and the
one who cannot, gives up his independence and lives under
the protection of some warrior's sword. Its woof is com-
merce. The means to this civilisation is the sword, its auxiliary. is courage and strength, and its aim is enjoyment here
and hereafter.

Quite different was the case where we of the Aryan civilisation of India went. The place of the sword was placed at the
feet of Dharma and the weak. The wielder of it, the Kshatriya,
was the protector of the weak and the law of righteous living.
The Western Pandit propounded a theory that the Aryans
came from somewhere outside, and conquered and enslaved
the original inhabitants of this country. Beyond the Wester-

ner's desire to draw a parallelism between what he has done and the conduct of the Aryan, there is not a shred of evidence for such a theory. The Rig Veda, the earliest literature of the A yans, nowhere states directly or indirectly that the Aryans came from anywhere outside. If Ramayana is an evidence of the Aryan expansion, we find that Rama, who may be taken as representing the Aryan, only allies himself with the powers of the south. He never annihilates any people. The means adopted for expansion by the Aryan was division into Varnas while that of the European civilisation is the sword. The object of the Europeans is to exterminate all, in order that they may themselves live comfortably. The aim of the Aryans is to raise all upto their own level or even to a higher one. "In Europe it is victory everywhere for the strong and death to the weak. In the land of Bharata, every social rule is for the protection of the weak."

THE GREAT TEACHERS OF THE WORLD*

The Necessity for a Mutiplicity of Prophets and Incarnations

Just as the universe is moving in cycles of wave forms, the spiritual life of nations too is subject to an upward and downward movement in the course of their history. When the spiritual life of a people has degraded to a very low level, it again gains strength and rises into a tidal wave, at the crest of which is found a shining soul who is both the creator of that rise as also at the same time a creature of it. In other words, he is the product of the people's heritage, and at the same time, it is he who gives dynamism to the life of the people and raises them to a high state of attainment. These are called the great World Teachers or Prophets or the World's Messengers of Light or the Incarnations of God.

In the light of this theory the idea of some that there can be only one religion and one Prophet is incorrect. From the lives of these great men, we find that each of them was destined to play a part, and a part only in the world's history. The influence of a Prophet rules society for an age and he is succeeded in time by another. It is the totality of the contributions of all of them that creates the great harmony. Almost the majority of men requires a personal religion. Principles they may talk in theory, but they can understand it only when it is embodied in a personality. So you find a vast majority of mankind worshipping Godmen or Incarnations of God. Christians, Buddhists and Hindus do it openly, but the Muslims, who do not practise the worship of their Prophet, have ended by becoming the worshippers of innumerable

---

*Vol. IV, p. 116. Delivered at California.

saints. Christ, the God-man, said, "He that hath seen me hath seen the Father." God, as an Impersonal Principle, is everywhere but we are so constituted at present that we can see Him, feel Him, only in and through a human God. These are the Incarnations. They do not come to the world as often as we, but they come for a mission which they have to fulfil. Being messengers, they do not reason out what they teach. They teach out of their direct perception without groping in the dark as we do. They believe in themselves, as they are aware of their direct base in God. As they speak out of realisation, their words are direct and charged with power. Some of the greatest of them even teach through silence. There is an old Sanskrit verse which says: "I saw the teacher sitting under a tree. He was a young man of sixteen and the disciple was an old man of eighty. The preaching of the Teacher was silence, and the doubts of the disciple departed."

These great teachers are the living gods on earth. Whom else should we worship? They are higher than any conception of God that we could form, because the ideas we could form of all divine attributes like mercy, forgiveness, freedom, etc, will be limited and distorted by our own littleness. "Talking about God and the Impersonal and this and that is all very good; but these Man-gods are real gods of all nations and all races. These divine men have been worshipped, and will be worshipped so long as man is man. Of what avail is a mere mystical principle?"

The quarrels between the followers of these different Prophets have arisen not out of knowledge of their teachings but out of ignorance. About those who think that man can understand the Truth or the Divinity or God only through one Prophet in the world, we have to conclude that they do not understand the divinity in anybody. They are like those

who drink brackish water from a well, because the well was
dug by their 'fathers.

"Now in my little experience I have collected this knowledge—that for all the devilry that religion is blamed for,
religion really is not at all at fault; no religion ever persecuted
men; no religion ever burned witches; no religion ever did any
of these things. What is it that made people do all these?
Politics and never religion; and if such politics takes the name
of religion, whose fault is that?"

In religion also what scientists call atavism, reverting
to the old, can happen. But to merely get stagnated in our
ideas is like becoming lifeless like a wall. Only when we
begin to think for ourselves, we are really born in the world
of religion. "Be active in thought, and wherever there is
activity there must be difference. Difference is the sauce of
life; it is the beauty, it is the art of everything. Difference
makes all beautiful here. It is variety that is the source of life,
the sign of life. Why should we be afraid of it? Those who
understand this will easily grasp that all the great messengers
and prophets were great and true, and will not owe allegience
to a particular Prophet alone to the exclusion of all others.

The Message of Krishna

Taking the Prophets of India, let us look at Krishna's
message. He taught not to be attached to anything in the
world because everything in the world is continually changing
and will ultimately desert us. So be attached to God only.
In other words love Him only. For, God never changes and
never deserts us. He also taught that man should never
abandon his duties. All works are to be done as offering
unto the Lord. "Whoever lives in the midst of the world,
and works, and gives up all the fruits of his actions unto the
Lord, he is never touched with the evils of the world." Just

as the lotus born under the water rises up and blossoms above the water, even so is the man who is engaged in the activities of the world giving up all the fruits of his activities unto the Lord. When all duties are done as an offering unto the Lord, no work is low or menial. "Each man's work is quite as good as that of the emperor on the throne." Go forward and do not pay too much attention to the nature of the work you have to do. Ask your mind if you are unselfish. If you are, never mind anything, nothing can resist you. Plunge into the duty at hand, and when you have done this, by degrees you will realise the truth: "Whosoever in the midst of intense activity finds intense peace, whosoever in the midst of peace finds the greatest activity, he is a Yogi, he is a great soul, he has arrived at perfection." The implication of the teaching is that no duty in the world deserves to be called menial. All the duties of the world are sacred.

The Message of the Buddha

Next comes the tremendous message of the Buddha. He says, "Root out selfishness; be not of the world." A worldly man will think he will be unselfish but when he looks at the face of his own wife or child and thinks of their interest, selfishness overcomes him. Then his watchword will be: "I first, and let everyone else look out for himself." So the Buddha advises the abandonment of all worldly ties and asks us to think of the misery of the millions of the world involved in it.

While this is true, Krishna's message also must have a place. Unless we take up that message of work without attachment, we cannot conscientiously and with peace, joy and happiness perform any duty in our lives.

The Message of Christ

Next comes the message of the prophet of Nazareth. He declares, "Be ready, for the kingdom of Heaven is at hand." It means, do not delay a moment, leave nothing for tomorrow, get ready for the final event which may overtake you immediately, even now.

The Message of Mohammed

And then comes Mohammed, the messenger of equality, the brotherhood of all Mussalmans. Some people see no good in his teachings, but they forget that his message could not then have survived and become a force in the world. Mohammed stood for the idea that there should be equality among all Muslims irrespective of race, caste, creed or colour. While Hindus teach a grand philosophy, they are deficient in the practice of equality of all. The world requires the message of all these prophets and everyone must strive to become a prophet himself.

MY MASTER*

The Occidental and the Oriental Ideals of
Civilised Life

Whenever this world requires a moral adjustment, a wave of power comes to do this. As man lives on two planes, the spiritual and the material, this power works on both these fields. On the material plane, in modern times, the West has been the field of all developments, while Asia has been the spring of all forces in the spiritual plane throughout history. Today when materialism is in its height of glory and man is likely to forget his divine nature through his grave dependence on matter, a new spiritual adjustment has become necessary. The power that does this has been set in motion, and that at no distant date, will bring on mankind once more the memory of its real nature. The place from which it will start again will be Asia. The present adjustment will be through the harmonising or the mingling of the two ideals of life represented by the occidental and the oriental. The oriental finds in the world of the Spirit all that makes the world real for him—all that he wants and hopes for. To the occidental standing for material power, he appears a dreamer. So does the oriental look upon the occidental as a childish dreamer, as he is engrossed in the ephemeral toys of worldly power and possessions which are only for a few days. But the Oriental ideal is as necessary for the progress of the human race as is the Occidental, probably the former more. Machines have never made man happy, only the man who has mastered the mind can become so. Why should a man who can send a current of electricity through a wire

*Vol. IV, p. 154.

be called a very great man and a very intelligent man? Does not Nature do a million times more than that every moment? Why not then fall down and worship Nature? What avails if you have power over the whole world, if you have mastered every atom in the universe? That will not make you happy unless you have the power of happiness in yourself, until you have conquered yourself. Nature does not mean mere external nature, however grand and impressive it may be. There is the internal nature of man transcending the external, and in the conquest of it the Oriental excels just as the occidental does in regard to the conquest of external nature. So to learn about the mysteries of spiritual life, about God, Atman etc., the aspirant should sit at the feet of the Orient, just as the Orient has to go to the Occident to know the ways of mastering external nature.

To understand the life of this great man Sri Ramakrishna, who has set in motion such a wave of spirituality in India, you have to understand, first of all, what India really stands for. People who are blinded with the glamour of material things, whose lives are dedicated to eating and drinking and enjoying, whose ideal of pleasure is in the senses—if such people go to India, they will see it but as a land of poverty, squalour, superstition, darkness and hideousness everywhere. For the minds of such observers, enlightenment means dress, riches, education and polite social etiquettes. But they forget that there in India alone live men who did not go beyond their frontiers to conquer and plunder other people, whose only fault was that they accumulated wealth by the hard labour of their hands which tempted other nations to come and despoil them. In return for such depredations, they want to send to the world the visions of the Supreme and the knowledge of the secrets of human nature. They know that behind materialism is the real nature of man which no sin can tarnish, no crime can spoil, no fire can burn, no weapons can kill. To them, this true spiritual nature of man is as real as any material object is to the senses of the Occidental. Just as you ar heroic in the name of patriotism and ready to give up your lives for the country, so are they in the name of God. Among them you get men who, learning that the world is an appearance, are ready to give up all their property and spend their lives in contemplation. Their heroism lies in that they are ready to face death, because they are convinced there is no death for them as Spirit. This conviction has made them invincible through hundreds of years of oppression by foreign invaders and tyrants. Being such a nation, they have produced spiritual giants, even in the days of direst disaster.

The Cultural Milieu in India in the Mid-nineteenth Century

Now in the beginning of the nineteenth century, when Western influence began to pour into India, subsequent to the conquest by the organised might of the West, doubts began to arise in the minds of the Indian intelligentia about the foundations of their civilisation. A section of people arose who felt the whole national existence up to then had been a failure, and they must begin anew on the Occidental plan, "tear up their old books, burn their philosophies, drive away their teachers and break down their temples." Instead of driving away superstition and making a real search for truth, they came to think that the test of truth is: "What does the West say?" Out of this feeling of unrest arose a wave of so-called reform, which meant only condemnation of the past of India and imitation of Western ways. But they were unaware of the secret of India's continued existence in the world in spite of the ordeals through which the country had passed. "The Indian nation cannot be killed. Deathless it stands,

and it will stand so long as that spirit shall remain in the
background, so long as our people do not give up their spirituality. Beggars they may remain, poor and poverty-stricken,
dirt and squalour may surround them perhaps throughout
all time, but let them not give up their God, let them not
forget that they are the children of the sages......So long
as holiness is supremely venerated, India cannot die."

Sri Ramakrishna and His Spiritual Quest

It was then when these reform-movements were inaugurat-
ed in India that a child was born of poor Brahmana parents on
the 18th of February 1836 in a remote village of Bengal.
The parents of this boy, who became my Master, were supreme
examples of real Brahmana orthodoxy, which, even though set
in a surrounding of exclusiveness, is based upon non-covet-
ousness, continuous asceticism and charity to all even at
one's own expense. "Of them this child was born, and he
was a peculiar child from boyhood. He remembered his
past from his birth and was conscious for what purpose he
came to the world, and every power of his was devoted for
fulfilment of that purpose."

While he was quite young, his father died. As he grew
up, he was sent to a school by his guardians. A Brahmana
boy has to get educated in order that he may follow a
learned profession. In his early days the boy attended a
conference of learned men that met in a rich man's house and
found that the only purpose of the type of learning they
possessed was to get some money and a few pieces of cloth.
It roused in him very early in life a repugnance   to the type of
learning imparted in schools and a resolve to pursue spiritual
knowlege rather than acquire such secular learning. He therefore neglected his studies. But the family being very poor, he
had to migrate to Calcutta in course of time, and he became a

temple priest there. The Deity installed in the temple was the
blissful Divine Mother. As the boy conducted the worship
morning and evening, this one idea came to fill his mind—
"Is there anything behind this image? Is it true that there
is a Mother of bliss in the universe? Is it true that She lives
and guides this universe? Or is it all a dream? Is there any
reality in religion?"

This kind of noble scepticism based on the yearning to
know whether the truths of religion are factual or not, comes
to the Hindu mind, and to get a convincing answer for it,
the Hindus, through the ages, have been ready to sacrifice
themselves and everything in life. It cannot be satisfied by
mere intellectual understanding, a mere rationalistic com-
prehension. Reasoning yields only probabilities and nothing
more. The Hindu mind demands something much more convincing—intense realisation that is much more real than this
world is to our senses. To one possessed of this feeling, every
moment spent on other occupations, however noble, is time
wasted. Life and all its experiences are momentary and yield
no ultimate meaning for our existence. The solution can be
found only in God and in religion. If these are true, life
becomes explained, life becomes bearable, becomes enjoyable;
otherwise life is but a useless burden. "Mere reasoning
however cannot take us very near it. We have to sense God
to be convinced that there is a God. We must sense the
facts of religion to know that they are facts. Nothing else
and no amount of reasoning, but our own perceptions can
make these things real to us, can make my belief firm as a
rock."

This idea took possession of the boy and his whole life
became concentrated upon that. Day after day, he would be
weeping and saying, "Mother, is it true that Thou existest
or is it all poetry? Is the blissful Mother the imagination of

the misguided poets or is She a reality?" Because he had no formal education of a university, his mind was original and he made therefore a direct search for Truth than go to other people's collection of thoughts in books. Now this quest whether God can be tangibly seen became uppermost in his mind and it gained such strength that he could not do anything external in life, including external worship. So absorbed he became in this spiritual quest. A mood of this type, thought not so strong, may come to many of us in times of despair and depression, but the animal man in us shakes all that off, and "down we go, animal man once more, eating and drinking and dying, and dying and drinking and eating, again and again." But this boy was exceptional. The quest became so intense that, "as he told me many times, he could not tell when the sun rose or set or how he lived. He lost all thought of himself and forgot even to eat......Then a whole day would pass, and towards the evening, when the peal of bells in the temples and the voices singing would reach the wood, it would make the boy very sad, and he would cry, 'Another day is gone in vain, Mother, and Thou hast not come. Another day of this short life has gone, and I have not known the Truth.' In the agony of his soul, sometimes he would rub his face against the ground and weep, and this one prayer burst forth, 'Do Thou manifest Thyself to me. Thou Mother of the universe, see that I need Thee and nothing else."

True to his resolution to abandon everything in order to have the Mother, he banished from his mind every idea of possession and could not even touch money. "This may appear to be something occult but even in after-life, if I touched him, while sleeping, with a piece of money, his hand would become bent and his whole body would become, as it were, paralysed." Just like possession, he abandoned sexuality, the other obstacle in the way of man's spiritual advancement.

For him every woman represented the Mother and he could not think of her in mere sex relation.

Later on, speaking about his tremendous thirst after God, he said to me: "My child, suppose there is a bag of gold in one room, and a robber in the next room; do you think that the robber can sleep? He cannot. His mind will be always thinking how to get into that room and obtain possession of that gold. Do you think that a man who is firmly persuaded that there is a Reality behind all these appearances, that there is a God, that there is One who never dies, One who is infinite Bliss, a Bliss compared with which these pleasures of the senses are simply play things—can he rest content without struggling to obtain Him, can he cease his efforts for a moment? No, he will become mad with longing." Literally he was seized with a divine madness. When worldly-minded men who did not understand its source saw him, they dubbed him as one out of mind. It is natural for those who are seized with the reality of world's vanities, to consider one who is quite unlike themselves as out of mind.

Arrival of Teachers

Days, weeks and months passed thus in continuous struggle until visions of Truth began to dawn on him, as veil after veil was, as it were, taken off from his mind. To him at this critical juncture came a teacher, a learned woman, a Sannya-sini, whom the Mother Herself seemed to have sent to him. She remained near the boy for several years, taught him the forms of traditional worship, initiated him in the different paths of Yoga and thus guided and brought into harmony this tremendous river of spirituality in him. She declared to all his detractors that they considered him mad only because he was not mad like themselves after worldly possessions and pleasures. Those who are mad after these transient worldly attainments are the really mad people, and not one who sought the eternal Being.

Sometime later came to him another teacher, a wandering Sannyasin. He was an idealist who did not accept the reality of the world, and in demonstration of this, always lived in the open, never going under a roof in storm or sunshine. Under his instruction, the boy came to realise the truth of the Vedanta in a short time. He was also initiated into the Order of Sannyasins by him.

Marriage and After

Sometime earlier, when he was passing through the spiritual storm and many took him to be unbalanced in mind, his relatives had taken him to his village home and married him to a girl of very tender years, considering that this would have a balancing effect on his life. But soon after, when he returned to Calcutta, he again fell into his mood of spiritual inebriation. He forgot everything about home, marriage and wife. After some years when this girl had grown into a young woman in her village home, she was seized with anxiety to hear from the village people that her husband had gone mad. So thinking that it was her duty to be with him and serve him in that condition, she came to Calcutta from the distant village, walking all the way. Usually one who takes to the life of Sannyasa is thereby free from all worldly obligations, but "this young man fell at the feet of his wife and said, 'As for me, the Mother has shown that She resides in every woman and so I have learned to look upon every woman as Mother. That is the one idea I can have about you. But if you wish to drag me to the world as I have been married to you, I am at your service." The maiden was pure and noble-minded. She understood and sympathised with her husband's aspirations. She told him, 'that she had no desire to drag him down to worldliness and all that she wanted was to remain near him, serve him and learn of him.' She thus became one of his most devoted disciples, always revering him as a divine being.

Other Spiritual Practices

Next, the desire to know the Truth of various religions seized upon his soul. In India to know the truth of a religion does not mean mastering its theory but realising the truth it conveys. He found a Mohammedan saint of this type and underwent the discipline prescribed by him, and found that those devotional methods led him to the same goal he had already attained. He did the same with the true religion of Jesus the Christ too. Thus from actual experience, he came to know that the goal of every religion is the same, the difference being largely in method and still more in language, and that the quarrels among them are only due to the pursuit of selfish purposes by their followers. Next he wanted to learn true humility, which means 'not me but Thou'. Being wonderfully practical, he wanted to realise this in a literal sense. The method he adopted for this was to do the menial work of cleaning the house of a Pariah—a community whom the Hindus in general shunned as unclean and untouchable. The Pariah would not, however, allow him to do this as he believed it would bring on himself great sin. So Ramakrishna would secretly enter his house at night and wipe the place with his long hair and pray to the Divine Mother saying, "O my Mother! Make me the servant of the Pariah, make me feel that I am even lower than the Pariah."

Among the various other kinds of Sadhanas he practised was his effort to efface the idea of sex from the mind and thus realise that the soul is sexless. For this he dressed like a woman and lived like a woman in a household among women.

Thus he overcame the idea of sex. Not only that, he learnt to recognise the Blissful Mother in every woman irrespective of her character. I have myself seen him falling at the feet of fallen women saying, "Mother, in one form Thou art in the street and in another form Thou art the universe. I salute Thee, Mother, I salute Thee."

As a Teacher

After having thus gained unsullied purity, the time came for him to give to humanity what he had learnt. But his method of teaching was peculiar. Being a very highly venerated person, people gathered around him in large numbers, but here was a teacher "who had no thought whether he was respected or not. He had not the least idea that he was a great teacher. He thought that it was Mother who was doing everything and not he." He sought no one. He expressed his idea of teaching by his famous illustration: 'When the lotus opens, the bees come of their own accord to seek the honey. So let the lotus of your character be full blown and the results will follow. He alone teaches who has something to give, for teaching is not talking, teaching is not imparting doctrines, it is communicating. Spirituality can be communicated just as really as I can give a flower. This is true in the most literal sense.' He spoke in patois—the unpolished dialect of villagers. But every word of it was forceful and instinct with light, for it was not what is spoken, much less the language in which it is spoken, but it is the personality of the speaker that dwells in everything he says, that carries weight."

He criticized no one. For years I lived with him, but never did I hear those lips utter one word of condemnation on any sect. He had the same sympathy for all the sects; he had found the harmony between them.

God Can be Experienced

He came to live near Calcutta, an important university town in our country, which was then sending out sceptics and materialists by hundreds every year. "I heard of this man and I went to hear him. He looked just like an ordinary man with nothing remarkable about him......and I thought, 'Can this man be a great teacher?' I crept near to him and asked him the question which I had been asking others all my life, 'Do you believe in God, Sir?' 'Yes' he replied. 'Can you prove it, Sir?' I asked, and 'Yes,' came his reply. 'How?' I asked; and he replied, 'Because I see Him just as I see you here, only in a much intenser sense'. That interested me at once. For the first time, I found a man who dared to say that he saw God, that religion was a reality to be felt, to be sensed in an infinitely more intense way than we can sense the world. I began to go to that man day after day, and I actually saw that religion could be given. One touch, one glance can change the whole life." I have read about this in the lives of the spiritual luminaries of the past and now "when I myself saw this man doing this, all scepticism was brushed aside. It could be done and my Master used to say, 'Religion can be given and taken more tangibly, more really, than anything else in the world......Religion consists in realisation ....The first ideal of this attempt to realize religion is that of renunciation. Darkness and light, enjoyment of the world and enjoyment of God, will never go together.... Bit by bit we must go towards it.' "

Harmony of Religions

"The second idea that I learnt from my Master and which is perhaps the most vital, is the wonderful truth that the religions of the world are not contradictory or antagonistic;

they are but various phases of the one Eternal Religion; that, one Eternal Religion is applied to various planes of existence is applied to the opinions of various minds and various races." Nature is unity in variety. So long as there are different natures, different types of men and cultures in this world, the same religious truth will require different adaptations. "The only true teacher is he who can convert himself, as it were, into a thousand persons at a moment's notice. The only teacher is he who can immediately come down to the level of the student and transfer his soul to the student's soul and see through the student's eyes and hear through his ears and understand through his mind. Such a teacher can really teach religion, and none else."

There is a spurious way of universal acceptance of religions. It is the patronising way which we see some people adopting. To call all these religions as ethical, having some good things, or to think that all religions are but little bits of pre-historic evolution but ours is a fulfilment of things—these attitudes cannot be called true religious liberalism. We have to recognise that each one of them has the same saving power as the others. "The same God answers all and it is not you or I or any body of men that is responsible for the safety and salvation of the least little bit of the soul; the same Almighty God is responsible for all. I do not understand how people declare themselves to be believers in God and at the same time think that God has handed over to a little body of men all truth and that they are the guardians of the rest of humanity. How can you call that religion? Religion is realisation, not mere talk, mere trying to believe, mere groping in darkness, mere parroting the words of ancestors and thinking of it as religion, mere making political something out of the truths of religion—this is not religion at all......Wherever there is a man trying to realise religion, from his lips have come the

fiery words: 'Thou art the Lord of all. Thou art in the heart
of all. Thou art the guide of all. Thou art the teacher of all,
and Thou carest infinitely more for the good of Thy children
than we can ever do.' "

Renunciation as the Soul of His Life and Teaching

In the presence of my Master I found out that man could
be perfect, even in this body. His lips never criticized anyone.
His eyes were beyond the possibility of seeing evil, and his
mind beyond the capacity of thinking evil. This tremendous
purity, this tremendous renunciation is the one secret of all
spirituality. The more the trait of renunciation lessens in an
individual or a group of people, the more will the senses creep
into the field of religion and destroy spirituality. My Master
was the embodiment of renunciation. There were many who
pressed him to accept rich presents, but these were the only
men from whom he would turn away. He was an eample
of the complete conquest of lust and desire for wealth. "It is
necessary in a time like this that a man should arise to demonstrate to the sceptics of the world that there breathes one who
does not care a straw for all the gold or all the fame that is in
the universe. Yet, there are such men."

Love of Fellow Beings

The other idea that he held forth in his life was intense
love of others. Men came in crowds to hear him and he
would talk even twenty hours in the twentyfour, and that not
for one day but several years and his body broke down under
the pressure of this tremendous strain. But yet he could not
be deterred from speaking even to the humblest of thousands
who sought his aid. Even when he was in the grip of severe

throat disease, he could not be restrained from these exertions. When expostulated with, he would reply, 'I do not care. I will give up twenty thousand such bodies to help one man.' Such was his love and compassion for others. When some one suggested to him that he should cure his ailment by the exercise of Yogic power, he replied, 'My friend, I thought you are a sage, but you talk like other men of the world. This mind has been given unto the Lord. Do you mean to say that I should take it back and put it upon the body, which is but a mere cage of the soul?' So he went speaking to spiritual enquirers without rest, saying, 'While I am able to speak, I must teach them.' One day he told us that he would lay down the body that day, and repeating the most sacred word of the Vedas, he entered into Samadhi and passed away."

He left behind a few boys who had renounced the world for the sake of God. Having had the contact of the blessed one for years, they stood their ground against the pinch of extreme poverty and antagonism of many. Gradually their effort in spreading the message of their Master all over India succeeded, and today, "the power of that man has spread beyond India, and if there has ever been a word of truth, a word of spirituality that I have spoken anywhere in the world, I owe it to my Master; only the mistakes are mine."

"This is the message of Sri Ramakrishna to the world. Do not care for doctrines, do not care for the dogmas or sects or churches or temples; they count for little compared with the Essence of Existence in each man, which is spirituality; and the more this is developed in a man, the more powerful is he for good. Earn that first, acquire that, and criticize no one; for all doctrines and creeds have some good in them. ....Only those who have attained to spirituality can com_ municate it to others, can be great teachers of mankind. They alone are the power of Light......To proclaim and make clear that fundamental unity underlying all religions was the mission of my Master.. He left every religion undisturbed, because he had realised that in reality they are all part and parcel of the one Eternal Religion."

HINDUISM AND SRI RAMAKRISHNA*

The Veda is the scripture of Hinduism, and all other scriptural texts like the Puranas, are called Smritis and their authority follows only as far as they follow the Vedas and do not contradict their authority. With regard to the whole collection included in the Veda, only those portions of it that do not refer to purely secular matters, and which do not merely record tradition or history, or merely provide incentive to duty, form the Veda in the real sense.

There are two main methods of knowing the Truth. The first consists in sense faculties and reasoning power, and the second in the subtle, super-sensuous power of knowledge without the aid of the senses. Knowledge obtained by the former is science, and by the latter, the Veda.

The whole body of super-sensuous truths, having no beginning and no end, and called by the name of the Veda, is ever-existent. The persons in whom the supersensuous power of understanding has developed discover these truths. Such discoverers of the spiritual truth are called the Rishis. Only one who has developed this power of supersensuous perception is a real teacher of religion.

The Vedas are divided into two portions—Jnana-kanda and Karma-kanda. The first is the knowledge portion, whose teachings are of eternal validity for the salvation of man, and the other is ritualistic portion whose application is limited within the world of Maya. All social laws and customs are based on Karma-kanda, but they have to change with changing times. "But when, by the process of time, fallen from the true ideals and rules of conduct and devoid of the spirit of renuncia-

_____

tion, and addicted only to blind usages and degraded in intellect, the descendants of the Aryas failed to appreciate the spirit of even the Puranas, which taught men of ordinary intelligence the abstruse truths of the Vedanta in concrete form and diffuse language, appearing antagonistic to one another on the surface because of each inculcating with special emphasis only particular aspects of the spiritual ideal—

"And when, as a consequence they reduced India, the fair land of religion, to a scene of almost infernal confusion by breaking up piecemeal the one Eternal Religion of the Vedas (Sanatana Dharma)—the grand synthesis of all aspects of the spiritual ideal—into conflicting sects, and by seeking to sacrifice one another in the flames of sectarian hatred and intolerance—

"Then it was that BhagawanSri Ramakrishna incarnated himself in India to demonstrate what the true religion of the Aryas is; to showwhere amidst all its many divisions and offshoots scattered over the land in the course of its immemorial history, lies the true unity of the Hindu religion, which by its overwhelming number of sects, discordant to the superficial view, quarrelling constantly with each other and abounding in customs divergent in every way, has constituted itself into a misleading enigma for our countrymen and the butt of contempt for foreigners; and above all to hold up before men, for their lasting welfare, as a living embodiment of Sanatana Dharma, his own wonderful life into which he infused the universal spirit and character of this Dharma, so long cast into oblivion by the process of time.

"In order to show how the Vedic truths, eternally existent as instruments with the Creator in His work of creation, preservation and dissolution, reveal themselves spontaneously in the minds of the Rishis purified from all impressions of worldly attachment, and because such verification and confir-

mation of the spiritual truths will help the revival, reinstate-
ment, and spread of religion—the Lord, though the embodiment of the Vedas, in this His new incarnation has thoroughly
discarded all external forms of learning."

India's history has been a succession of periods of decline
and revival. A period of decline has been succeeded by
one of revival of greater glory and power. Everytime our
country has fallen into a swoon, India's Lord, by the manifestation of Himself, has revivified her, revealing Himself more
and more in his successive Incarnations. The downfall
that India has sustained in the present age has been the most
dismal, compared with which the periods of decadence of
the past were of little consequence. But India is going to
revive from it and rise to a splendour outshining all her
achievements of the past. And as the sure pledge
of this glorious future, the all-merciful Lord has manifested
in the present age, as said before, as an Incarnation, which in
point of completeness in revelation, its synthetic harmonising
of all ideals, and its promoting of every sphere of spiritual
culture, surpasses the manifestation of all the past ages....
"With the conviction in your heart that·you are the servants
of the Lord, His children, His helpers in the fulfilment of His
purpose, enter the arena of work."

PAVHARI BABA*

The ideal is the more fundamental factor in life than the practical. The practical is only an approximation to it in everyday life. In spite of the difficulty of actualising the ideal, it should not be neglected or forgotten. For the ideal is the subtle aspect of things, their cause, and the practical is the effect, which is bound to manifest sometime or other under favourable conditions. Only a bit, a small bit, of infinite thought can be made to descend to the plane of matter. The rest will not allow itself to be accommodated in the sense plane. Man must raise himself to that higher plane if he wants to enjoy its beauties, to bathe in its light, to feel his life pulsating in unison with the causal state of the universe. The great ideal is put in the Gita, "He who finds rest in the midst of activity and activity in rest, he is the wise amidst men, he is the Yogi, he is the doer of all work." But few ever reach it, and we must be content to piece together the different aspects of human perfection developed in individuals.

"In religion we have the man of intense thought, of great activity in bringing help to others, the man of boldness and daring self-realisation, and the man of meekness and humility." The subject of this sketch was a man of the latter type—a man of wonderful humility and intense self-realisation. Born of Brahmana parentage at Guzi near Banares, he came as a mere boy to stay with his uncle at Ghazipur. His uncle was a Naishthika Brahmacharin or one under the vow of life-along celibacy. He belonged to the Ramanuja sect known as Sri Sampradaya. The Hindu ascetics are divided into the main divisions of Sannyasins, Yogins, Vairagins and

---

*Vol. IV, p. 283.

Panthis. The Sanyasins follow Advaitism of Sankaracharya.
The Yogins, though following Advaita, specialise in practising
different types of Yoga. The Vairagins are the dualistic
disciples of Ramanujacharya and others. The Panthis are
Orders founded in later days during Muslim rule.

Not much is known about Pavhari Baba's early life except
that he was a diligent student of Vyakarana and Nyaya and the
theology of his sect. He was a lively boy with a remarkable
aptitude for learning languages. There was nothing then
foreshadowing the tremendous seriousness of his later life.

Then something happened which made the young scholar
feel the serious import of life. His uncle passed away, thus
eliminating from his life the only person on whom his love was
concentrated. The craving for something in religion which
is more than mere booklore dawned in his mind, and he went
as a wandering ascetic in search of a Guru and to get direction
on the mysteries of inner life. We know very little of his
travels, but from his knowledge of the Dravidian languages in
which a good deal of the literature on his sect is written, as
also with the old Bengali of the Vaishnavas of Sri Chaitanya's
Order, we can infer that he had spent much time in Southern
India and Bengal. It is known from the friends of his youth
that he visited the Mount of Girnar in Kathiawar where he
was initiated into the mysteries of practical Yoga by a Guru.
This Mount Girnar was very holy to the old Buddhists and
at its foot is a huge rock on which is inscribed an edict of
Ashoka. Girnar is sacred to Hindus also. It is believed
that it was sanctified by the stay of the great Avadhuta
Dattatreya. It was also believed that perfected Yogins can
be met there by the fortunate.

The next turning point in this young ascetic's life took
place when he became the disciple of a Sannyasin who prac-

tised Yoga also and lived on the banks of the Ganges near
Banares where he lived in a hole dug in the high banks of the
river. In later life, Pavhari Baba also followed this example
of the Guru. Yogins are noted for their liking for caves
where the temperature is even and sounds will not disturb
them. We also learn that he was learning the Advaita system
under a Sannyasin in Banares.

After years of travel, study and discipline, he came back
to his place at Gazipur where he was brought up. He was
now a transformed man in many respects. He was welcomed
by some of his old companions who had all by this time
become men of the world. They welcomed him and though
they could not understand him, they instinctively respected
him.

Now his peculiar habits of life began to develop one after
another. He dug a cave in the ground first like that of the
ascetic of Banares, and began to remain there for hours and
practise awful dietary discipline. The whole day he worked
in his little Ashrama, conducted the worship of Ramachandra
and cooked good dinners, the whole of which he distributed
among his friends and the poor. The service of all was an
act of worship of the Supreme for him. When everyone
had gone to sleep, the young ascetic would cross the Ganges
by swimming, and there on the other shore spend his whole
night in meditation and prayers and come back before day-
break. This routine of his continued for many days. His
diet was reduced gradually to a handful of bitter Margosa
leaves and a few pads of fried pepper. Then he gave up
going across the Ganga and began to live more and more in
the cave. It is said that for days and months he would be in
the cave absorbed in meditation without coming out. As
nobody knew on what he subsisted upon during those long
intervals, people came to call him Pavhari Baba or the 'air-

eating father.' Once, when he spent a very long time inside the cave, people gave him up as dead. But the Baba emerged and gave a feast to a large number of Sadhus. When not absorbed in meditation, he used to live in a room above the mouth of his cave. There he would receive the visitors. His fame gradually began to spread far and wide.

As in the case of many saints of India, there was no striking external activities in his life. For like many Indian saints he was averse to preach; for he knew that only internal discipline leads to truth and not words. Religion for them is no motive to social conduct but an intense search after, and realisation of, Truth in this very life. The present writer (i.e. Swamiji himself) had occasion to ask the saint why he did not come out of the cave to help the world, and in reply he gave out with his characteristic humility a humorous story. A criminal who had his nose cut for some offence, wanted to hide his noseless features to the world and so fled to a forest. He sat there on a tiger skin feigning meditation. Gradually be became famous as an ascetic and many began to gather round him. One enthusiastic young man persistently requested him to make him his disciple and to give him initiation. So the noseless saint asked him to get a sharp razor and come to a solitary place for his initiation. He took the razor from the hands of the young man and with one stroke cut off his nose, telling "This has been my initiation into the Order. I give it to you and you may diligently transmit it to others." Thus the sect of nose-cut saints spread all over the country. "Do you want me," the Baba asked, "to be the founder of another such sect?" Later, in a more serious mood, he said, "Do you think that physical help is the only help possible? Is it not possible for one mind to help other minds even without the activity of the body?" When he was asked on one occasion why a great Yogi like him should perform ritualistic

fire-sacrifice, worship the image of Sri Raghunathji etc.,
which are considered practices for beginners, his reply was,
"Why do you take for granted that everybody performs
Karma for his own good? Could not one perform Karma
for others?"

A thief once stole several articles from his Ashrama.
When he had bundled all the things, he saw the saint. Being
frightened to be found out, he dropped the bundle and began
to run away. Thereupon the saint, taking up the bundle in
his hand, pursued the thief to a considerable distance and
overtook him. Then with tears in his eyes, he begged the
thief's pardon for his intrusion and begged him to accept the
goods which he was in need of and which belonged to him
more than to himself. He was once bitten by a cobra. He
revived from the effect of the poison and, when asked about
the occurrence by his friends, his reply was that he was bitten
by the cobra, 'a messenger from the Beloved.' All physical
ailments he took only as messengers from the Beloved,
though he suffered intensely from them. Through his silent
love and gentleness, he exercised a great, unspoken influence
in the surrounding villages.

One of his great peculiarities was his great absorption
in the task on hand. He thus bestowed the same amount
of care and attention on cleansing a pot as in the worship
of Sri Raghunathji. His motto was this: "The means should
be loved and cared for as if it were the end itself." He was a
picture of humility. But it was not of the nature of weakness
and self-abasement. His humility was based on the realisation, as he himself expressed, of the idea contained in the
verse, 'O King! The Lord is the wealth of those who have
nothing—yes, of those who have thrown away all desire
for possession, even for that of one's own soul.' So he would
never teach directly, assuming the role of a teacher. But

once the spring was touched, the fountain welled up with infinite wisdom, though the replies were all indirect.

In appearance he was tall and plumpy but looked much younger than his real age. He had only one eye. His voice was the sweetest I have ever heard.

For the last ten years or more of his life, he had withdrawn himself entirely from the gaze of man. A few potatoes and a little butter placed in front of his room would be taken in at night whenever he was not in Samadhi and was living above ground. When inside the cave, he did not require even this. He was thus a witness to the science of Yoga and the living example of purity and humility and love.

His coming out of Samadhi used to be indicated by the coming of smoke from his cell, a sign that he was performing Homa. One day smell of burning flesh came with the smoke from the cave. As the smoke and smell became intense, people broke open the door only to find that the great Yogi had offered his own body as his last oblation to his sacrificial fire. Knowing what he was, we can only suggest that the saint saw that his last moment had come, and not wishing to cause trouble to anyone even after death, performed this last sacrifice of an Arya in full possession of body and mind. "The present writer (the Swamiji himself) owes a deep debt of gratitude to the departed saint, and he dedicates these lines, however unworthy, to the memory of one of the greatest Masters he has loved and served."

THE BUDDHA'S MESSAGE*

Priests and Prophets

Buddhism is the most tremendous movement that the world has hitherto seen. Not content with its native land, it spread into Tibet, Persia, Asia Minor, Russia, Poland etc. Its mission reached also China, Korea and Japan. Through the channels opened by Alexander's empire, it went into the mediterranean world and into vast portions of Asia and Europe.

To understand Buddhism, one has to know the condition in the religious life of India at the time of its birth. Priests dominated the field of religion. As everywhere, the priests in India accepted a God, but that God can be approached only through them. It means you must accept their domination and pay them to their satisfaction for your spiritual welfare. This was accomplished through elaborate sacrificial rites. None but the priestly class was acquainted with their intricacies, and through various superstitious stories, men were persuaded to believe in all those claims on behalf of the sacrificial cult.

"But while the priests were flourishing, there existed also the poet-prophets, the Sannyasins." The Sannyasins had nothing to do with the priestly ceremonies. They preached that man must, at a stage of development, give up ceremonies and prepare for death taking to the life of renunciation, for which the Sannyasins stood. The Sannyasins, to some extent, combated the domination of the priests, but in course of time they too began to appeal to the superstitious tendencies of the people. Again prophets had to come to break the

*Vol. VIII, p. 92.

spell produced by the new priests. Thus the history of religion in India, and of the world at large, has been characterised by priests coming to dominate the religious life and prophets arising to challenge it.

Religious Life in India when the Buddha appeared

When the Buddha appeared, India was in one of those ages when priestcraft and sacrificial religion dominated the country, and the ordinary man had very little to sustain his spiritual life. He could not learn the Vedas. By rules and regulations religion had become much complicated and exclusive. The Buddha cut through all the excrescences and exclusiveness of priest-craft and preached a religion which was free from rituals and priestly intervention, and was open to all irrespective of their birth or status.   He taught the very gist of the philosophy of the Vedas.

His Doctrines

"His doctrine was this: Why is there misery in our life? Because we are selfish. What is the way out? It is through the giving up of the self.   The self does not exist. The phenomenal world, all that we perceive, is all that exists. There is nothing called the soul underlying the cycle of life and death.   There is the stream of thought; one thought following another in succession, each thought coming into existence and becoming non-existent at the same moment. That is all.   There is no thinker of the thought, no soul. The body is changing all the time.   So is mind, consciousness. The self therefore is a delusion.   All selfishness comes because of holding on to the self, to the illusory self. If we know that in truth there is no self, then we will be happy and make others happy."

He lived what he preached. He preached against the sacrificial religion. If sacrificing an animal was good, it must be much mroe so if a man is sacrificed, and he offered himself in sacrifice to save an animal. God and soul are the two big superstitions. God is a superstition invented by priests. If there is a God, why is there so much misery in this world? Besides, He is bound by the law of creation. It is no good praying to or propitiating such a God. What is required is to kill the self. This is done by becoming unselfish and being ready to give up one's life even for the good of an ant. "Work not for any superstition, not to please any God, not to get any reward, but because you are seeking your own release by killing the self. Worship and prayer and all that—these are all nonsense. You say 'I thank God'— but where does He live? You do not know and yet you are all going crazy about God."

"Hindus can give up every thing except their God. To deny God is to cut off the ground from under the feet of devotion. And here, in the teaching of the Buddha, are no God and no soul—but simply work. What for? Not for the self, for the self is a delusion. We shall be ourselves when this delusion is vanished. Very few are there in the world that can rise to that height and work for work's sake.

Yet the religion of Buddha spread fast. It was because of the marvellous love which, for the first time in the history of humanity, overflowed a large heart and devoted itself to the service not only of all men but of all living things—a love which did not care for anything except to find a way of release from suffering for all beings.

"Man was loving God and had forgotten all about his brother man. The man who in the name of God can give up his very life, can also turn around and kill his brother men in the name of God. That was the state of the world.

They would sacrifice the son for the glory of God, but also would rob nations for the glory of God, and would drench the earth with blood for the glory of God. This was the first time they turned to the other God—man. It is man that is to be loved. It was the first wave of intense love for all men—the first wave of unadulterated wisdom—that starting from India, gradually inundated country after country, north, south, east and west."

The Buddha's idea was to turn man away from the superstitious idea of an extraneous God and of the numerous gods who bestow favours by propitiation and prayer, and not hard work. True prayer is not the mumbling of some words. It is participation in Divine Energy which is a constant affair. This universe is a constant prayer. But men in India at that time could not understand this higher meaning of prayer. As soon as it is introduced in an external sense it becomes a means for the introduction of priestcraft. So he wanted to bring about a revolutionary change; he brushed aside all seeking help from an external source and made man stand on his own feet. As a result of the Buddha's teaching, the sacrificial religion passed away from India.

Vedantic View contrasted with the Buddhist Teaching

The same truth, which the Buddha preached, the Hindus would like to teach in a positive way, without the denial of God and a spiritual self in man. It is this wise: "In the Upanishad there is already the great doctrine of the Atman and the Brahman. The Atman, the Self, is the same as Brahman, the Lord. Thus the Self is all that is. It is the only reality; Maya, delusion, makes us see it as different. There is one Self, not many. That one Self shines in various forms. Man is man's brother because all men are one.

A man is not only my brother, say the Vedas. He is my very self. Hurting any part of the universe, I only hurt myself. I am the universe. It is a delusion that I think I am Mr. so and so.... God exists; but He is not the man sitting upon a cloud. He is pure Spirit. Where does He reside? Nearer to you than your very self. He is the soul.... When you think of Him as some one separate from yourself, you do not know Him. He is yourself. That was the doctrine of the prophets of India."

Legacy of Buddhism

Buddhism has passed away from India. The cause of it is that there were many negative ideas in its teachings. In course of time his followers emphasised all those negative aspects, and the positive aspects were suffocated by negation. Too much emphasis on negation carries with it the danger of eventual destruction. The negative aspects of Buddhism—that there is no God and no soul—died, and in their place the positive Vedantic teaching that God is the one reality, prevailed. So the reformative elements of Buddha's teaching died out, but its formative, its positive, teachings survived. "Buddha taught kindness to all beings, including the lower ones. And since then there has not been a sect in India that has not taught charity to all beings, even to animals. This kindness, this mercy, this charity—greater than any doctrine—is what Buddhism left to us."

Besides, there is the personality of the Buddha, which is the noblest the world has seen. His life was dedicated to the service of fellow beings. He taught the Truth, because he found man in suffering, and he was moved by an urge to find out a way for him out of suffering. And when he found the way, he devoted his life and energies to show that way to mankind. Out of this love of his, sprang the greatest missionary effort of the ancient world. He claimed no distinction for himself, and never taught men to depend on him as a saviour. "Of all the teachers of the world, he was the one who taught us most to be self-reliant, who freed us not only from bondages of our false selves but from dependence on invisible beings or a being called God. He invited every one to enter into that state of freedom which he called Nirvana. All must attain to that one day; and that attainment is the complete fulfilment of man."

ON LORD BUDDHA*

Buddhism is one of the sects of India. Gautama, who came to be known as the Buddha, was disgusted with the state of religion in his time. Complicated ritualism, unending metaphysical disputations and claims of caste superiority based on birth, characterised the religious life of India at the time of his advent. He preached a religion in which the above mentioned three factors have no place. He stood against the sacrificial cult and in demonstration of it, offered himself as a sacrificial victim in place of a lamb. He gave no metaphysical theories about the Supreme Reality or the nature of God. To the question whether there is a God, he always gave an agnostic answer that he did not know. To those who spoke about God, he asked them to become pure and good like the God they preached. He claimed no speciality over other human beings for himself. The Buddhahood attributed to him is only a state which anyone can attain. He practised absolute renunciation and unselfish love for all, and he claimed this was all that is necessary for man's spiritual evolution. "He reached the same state of perfection to which others come by Bhakti, Yoga or Jnana." I do not endorse all his philosophy. I want a good deal of metaphysics, but there is no reasons why one should not see the beauty of this man who was bereft of all motive power, who never claimed himself to be an incarnation of God or a specially chosen prophet.

BUDDHISM, THE FULFILMENT OF
HINDUISM*

It has been just now said that I am going to criticize Buddhism. Far be it from me to criticize Him whom I worship as God incarnate on earth. While other countries of the world claim to follow the teachings of the Buddha we in India worship Him as God-incarnate on earth. Our point of difference is that the Buddha was not understood properly by his disciples. Like Jesus, the Sakya Muni came not to preach anything new, but for the fulfilment or the evolution of the religion of India. But the Buddhists failed to understand this. The religion of the Hindus has got two sections, the ceremonial and the spiritual. The spiritual teachings were at one time confined to the monks. The Sakya Muni, that is the Buddha, was himself a monk, and it was his glory "that he had the large-heartedness to bring out the truths from the hidden Vedas and throw them broadcast all over the world." He was the first great teacher in the world to bring missionarising into practise.

He was also the first teacher of the world to stand mainly for the ignorant and the poor. So he insisted that his teachings be given not in Sanskrit, the language of the learned, but in Pali, the tongue of the common people in his days.

Faith in a God, which the followers of Buddha assailed, is something that cannot be erased from the heart of man so long as there is death in the world and weakness in the human heart. On the philosophic side, the disciples of Buddha dashed themselves against the eternal rocks of the Vedas. Their teaching sought to take away from the nation "that

*Vol. I, p. 21.

eternal God to which every one, man or woman, clings so
fondly." The result was that Buddhism as a separate religion
had to die a natural death in India. By the disappearance
of Buddhism, the religious life of India also lost something
precious, that is, the reforming zeal and the wonderful sympathy and charity and the wonderful leaven which Buddhism
had brought into .the masses. "The Buddhist cannot stand
without the brain and philosophy of the Brahmana, nor the
Brahmana without the heart of the Buddhist. This separation
between the Buddhists and the Brahmanas is the cause
of the downfall of India."

CHRIST, THE MESSENGER*

The Necessity of a Humanised God

It has been said by Christ "No man hath seen God at any time, but through the Son." It means that the vibration of light is omnipresent, but you have to strike the light of the lamp before we can see the light. Even so the omnipresent God of the universe can be seen only when he is reflected by the giant lamps of the earth—the prophets, the man-Gods, the Incarnations, the embodiments of Divinity. We all know that God exists but we cannot understand Him. However-much we may try to form an ideal of God by ourselves, that conception will fall short of the ideal manifested in the character and personality of these great man-Gods. If they are higher than all our conceptions of God, what harm is there in worshipping such men as God? Not only is there no harm, but it is the only possible and positive way of wor-ship. Howevermuch we may struggle by means of abstrac-tions, our religion and our God can only be in terms of humanity. It is better to accept the actually existing thing than go after an idea which is only an abstraction. Hence, these Incarnations of God have been worshipped in all ages and in all countries.

The Background of Jesus Christ

In a study of the life of Jesus, who was a Jew by birth, we have to take account of the fact that the Jews of that time were passing through a state of cultural stagnation, of which the Pharisees and the Sadducees are examples. Such stagnation in the case of gifted people is only like the fall of

*Vol. IV, p. 138. Delivered at Los Angeles.

a wave preceding an upheavel that is to come later. At the time of the advent of Jesus, the proud and gifted race of Jews was hemmed all around by external enemies and driven to focus themselves in a centre surrounded by the Romans, the Hellenic intellectual tendencies and waves of thought from Persia, India and Alexandria. The race was forced to concentrate and focus all its energies upon Jerusalem and Judaism. When all power is once gathered and collected, it must burst into an expansion one day. The energy of this gifted race was also bound to burst on the world. The rise of Christianity was this expression and expansion of the concentrated energy of the Jewish race. It was on the surging wave of it that Jesus of Nazareth appeared. In him is embodied the best and the greatest in his own race, and in him was also the impetus for the future, not only to his own race but to unnumbered other races of the world.

Jesus Stood for Renunciation and Realisation

Now Jesus of Nazareth has got an occidental colouring in the hands of the European races where his religion has spread. But he was an oriental of orientals and his message was characterised by the oriental's yearning for the hereafter. The Western civilisation is an offspring of the Greek mentality, which was shaped by the beautiful but limited natural environment, and was intensely absorbed in the exploration and enjoyment of the limited environment that surrounded it. The Asiatic type, however, cast within the vast and limitless features of Nature, developed in another direction, learnt to look inside and not to the external. It became introspective in place of outward-going. It naturally wanted something that changes not, something which in the midst of the world of misery and death is eternal, blissful and undying. Jesus was the product of a culture shaped by such an environment and so his first watchword is, "Not this life, but something higher." Like the true Oriental, he lived for making his spiritual ideal practical. Westerners are no doubt practical in their own way—in military affairs, in managing political circles and such other worldly things. For them plans of salvation mean intellectual gymnastics, plans which are never worked out and never brought into practical life. For them the preacher who talks best is the greatest spiritual teacher. So in place of trying to understand Jesus in the light of his own teachings, many a Western intellectual has tried to make him a great politician or a great leader or a great patriotic Jew. But he says of himself "The foxes have holes, the birds of the air have nests, but the Son of Man hath not where to lay His head." Thus he stood for the idea of absolute renunciation. He had no idea of property, money or wealth, he had no family ties, he had no physical ideas in him, he had no sex ideas; he was a soul, nothing but the soul just working a body for the good of humanity. That was all his relation to the body. "The disembodied soul has no relationship to the animal, no relationship to the body. The ideal will be far away beyond us. But never mind, keep to the ideal. Let us confess that it is our ideal, but we cannot approach it yet."

Jesus was "the disembodied, unfettered, unbound Spirit. And not only so but he with marvellous vision had found that every man and woman, whether Jew or gentile, whether rich or poor, whether saint or sinner was an embodiment of the same undying Spirit as himself." Therefore the one work of his whole life was to call upon men to realise their own spiritual nature. Give up, he says, these superstitions, dreams that you are low and that you are poor. Think not that you are trampled upon and tyrannised over, as if you are slaves. Within you there is something that can never be tyrranised over, never be trampled upon, never be troubled, never be killed. You are all sons of God, the Immortal Spirit. "Know, the Kingdom of Heaven is within you", "I and my father are one." He never talks of this world except in so far as it is required to get hold of the world as it is, give it a push, and drive it forward and onward until the whole world has reached the effulgent Light of God.

Scholars in their higher criticism of the Bible have discussed how much of the New Testament is true. We are not concerned with it, and it does not matter whether the accounts of him were written only within 500 years of his birth and whether many facts mentioned are not historical. "But there must have been a nucleus, a tremendous power that came down, a marvellous manifestation of spiritual power." It stands there and it is what is adored as Jesus of Nazareth. There is only one way to worship him, and that is worshipping him as God and nothing else. Our scriptures say, "These great children of Light who manifest the Light themselves, who are Light themselves, they, being worshipped, become, as it were, one with us, and we become one with them."

Three Levels of Spiritual Teachings

Man worshipped the Divine in three ways according to his spiritual development.. All these ways are true just like photographs of the sun taken from different heights. For, humanity travels not from error to truth, but from truth to truth, or better, from lower truth to higher truth. In the religion of the unthinking masses all the world over, God is outside the universe, living in the Heaven and governing the world from there. He is the punisher of the bad and the rewarder of the good. When man advances intellectually and spiritually, he thinks of Him as Omnipresent and not distant. He is the soul of all souls; and those who develop still higher, they see God as Jesus puts it, "Blessed are the pure in the heart, for they shall see God." At last they find that they and the Father are one.

We find these three spiritual levels in the teachings of Jesus. In the common prayer he taught, "Our Father which art in Heaven, hallowed be Thy name." To a higher circle of people he gave the teaching, "I am in my Father and Ye in Me and I in you." And finally when the Jews asked him who he was, he declared that he and his Father were one.

The Spiritual Ideal of Jesus is today forgotten

The greatest lesson given by Jesus, which is also the basis of all religions, is renunciation. When a rich young man asked Jesus what he should do to gain eternal life, he asked him to sell all that he had, give it to the poor and follow him taking the cross. For, whoever gives up this life for His sake, finds the life immortal. What is meant by renunciation? It means unselfishness, which embodies the essence of all morality. A man established in unselfishness gives away his cloak also to the one who carries away his coat. "When a man has no more self in him, no possession, nothing to call 'me' or 'mine,' has given himself up entirely, destroyed himself as it were, in that man is God Himself, for in him self-will is gone, crushed out, annihilated. That is the ideal man." We may not all be able to reach anywhere near that ideal but let us not pull it down by compromises. Respect and worship the ideal and struggle towards it, though it may be with faltering steps.

Today the followers of Jesus have forgotten the ideal he stood for, superimposing on it a show of absolute respect for his personality. Suppose in the days when Jesus was preaching, a man approached him and said, 'I believe and accept all these principles that you are teaching. But I cannot accept you as the only begotten Son of God.' Surely Jesus would have replied, 'Follow the ideal and advance in your own way.' But his followers today have forgotten this—that he never cared for his self but wanted only to sacrifice himself for the uplift of all. He had no desire to be known by any. Quiet, unknown and silent he worked, just as the Lord works. But today his followers say, however perfectly unselfish you are, it is of no avail unless you give credit to our teacher. The disciples think that the Lord can manifest only once. There lies the whole mistake. For what has happened once could have happened before and could happen in future also. According to Hindu teachings as embodied in the Gita, "Wherever you find a great soul of immense power and purity struggling to raise humanity, know that he is born of my splendour and that I am there working through him. Let us therefore find God not only in Jesus of Nazareth but in all the great ones that have preceded him, and in all that came after him and in all that are yet to come."

NOTES FROM SEVERAL DISCOURSES
AND LECTURES

1. On Karma Yoga

As long as we require someone else to make us happy, we are slaves. So isolation of the Purusha from Prakriti and freedom from dependence on it is freedom or Kaivalya.

It is only work that is done as a free will offering to humanity and Nature that does not bring with it any binding attachment.

Duty of any kind is not to be slighted. The man who does what is considered a lower work, is not, for that reason alone, a lower man than he who does what is considered a higher work. A man should not be judged by the nature of his duties, but by the manner in which he does them. Every duty is holy and devotion to duty is the highest form of worship to God. It is certainly a source of great help in enlightening and emancipating the deluded and ignorance-encumbered souls, the bound ones.

Every successful man must have behind him somewhere tremendous integrity, tremendous sincerity, and that is the cause of signal success in life.

The great leaders of mankind belong to higher fields than the field of platform work.

The man who works through freedom and love cares nothing for results, but the slave wants his whipping and the servant his pay. Nothing is easier than to say "I work for work's sake", but nothing is so difficult to fulfil. There will be a motive somewhere—money, power or reputation.

We all find ourselves in the positions for which we are fit, each ball finds its own hole. If one has some capacity above another, the world will find that out in this universal adjustment that goes on. So it is no use to grumble.

2. On Fanaticism

There are fanatics of various kinds. Some people are wine fanatics and others cigar fanatics. They think that if man gave up smoking, the world would arrive at the millennium. Some fanatics in India think that if a woman could marry again when her husband is dead, it would cure all evil. There may be a man who goes about cheating people and with whom no woman is safe, but this scoundrel does not perhaps drink wine. He finds all goodness in that, and considers his wickedness as natural human frailty. In ninety cases out of a hundred, fanatics must be having bad livers or must be suffering from some kind of mental ailment. There are religious sects who run away from persecution for preserving liberty of conscience, but who, when they have themselves gained power, indulge in persecution of others.

All persecution is due to lack of confidence in a wise Providence. You must remember that the world has God to govern it and He has not left it to our charity. It is wise to avoid all sorts of fanatical reforms. Fanatics create only hatred. A fanatic is so, simply because he expects to get something in return. As soon as the battle is over, he goes for the spoil.

A man must not only have faith but intellectual faith too. To make a man take up everything and believe in it, would be to make him a fanatic.

3. Work is Worship

The highest man cannot work; for there is no binding element, no attachment, no ignorance in him. He is like a

ship, which, having gone over a mountain of magnet, has got
all its bolts and bars drawn out.

Men speak of helping the world because they have no
real faith in God. To them He is only G-O-D and nothing
more. How dare you arrogate to yourself the task of teaching
the architect of the universe, how to build. God has not fallen
into a ditch for you and me to help Him out by building hospi-
tals and such service institutions. The fact is that He allows
you to exercise your muscles in this great gymnasium, not in
order to help Him, but that you may help yourself. The
world goes on; you are but a drop in this ocean. A leaf
does not move, the wind does not blow without Him. Blessed
are we that we are given the privilege of working for Him,
not of helping Him. When you give a morsel of food to a dog,
think you are worshipping the dog as God; for God is that
dog. He is all, and is in all. Stand in that reverent attitude
to the whole universe, and then we shall attain perfect non-
attachment.

4. Work Without Motive

At the time when Gita was preached, there was a contro-
versy between those who performed Vedic ritualism involving
the sacrifice of many living creatures and the party opposed to
it who believed that gaining knowledge of the Self is the only
path to Moksha. Sri Krishna, the author of the Gita,
sought to resolve this dispute through his doctrine of work
without motive. Some think that the Gita is a later production,
added subsequently to the Mahabharata. This cannot be
correct, because the special teachings of the Gita are found
in every part of the Mahabharata.

Many nowadays think that working without motive
means not to be affected by pleasure and pain. But this
cannot be true, because it will make men stony-hearted,

and the worst criminals will have to be considered saints.

What the Gita has taught us is work with concentration on the higher self and forgetfulness of the lower ego. This is the meaning of working through Yoga. There are many functions of the body that we perform subconsciously and many others consciously. So also there can be work with the mind immersed in Samadhi, eliminating the small ego. This is what happens to some extent when a painter or an artist performs his best. His lower ego is then kept in abeyance. What the Gita teaches is that he who is one with the Lord through Yoga, performs all his works, immersed in concentration, and not looking for any personal benefit. Such work brings real good to the world.

All work is covered by some evil always, like fire by smoke. We should therefore do such work as brings the largest amount of good and the smallet measure of evil. Arjuna had to kill Bhishma, Drona etc. in battle. If he had not done that, the country would have been usurped by a body of proud and unrighteous kings to the great misfortune of the people.

Those who work without any consciousness of their lower ego are not affected by evil, for they work for the good of the world. To work without motive is to work unattached; that brings the highest bliss and freedom.

5. Sadhanas are Preparations for Higher Life

The attainment of super-consciousness is the goal of life. When that state is reached, this very man becomes free, and passes from this valley of 'life and death' to that one where death and life do not exist, and where we know the Real and become the Real. For attaining this, the first thing necessary

is a quiet and peaceful life. When we devote the whole day in
the struggle for existence, we cannot attain anything very high
in this life. If we have real aspiration, we may be born under
more propitious circumstances in the next life. Our environment adjusts itself to the intense needs we feel. In Nature
there are powers that correspond to our organic needs and
become operative when we really want them. So if you want
a really peaceful life, "that shall come—you may take that as
my experience". If it does not come in this life, it may come
in another. "You cannot have a strong desire if its object
were not outside for you already." But if you want to get it,
your craving for it must be as strong as that of a drowning
man for air.

"He who desires for a comfortable and nice life, and at the
same time wants to realise the Self, is like a fool who, wanting
to cross the river, caught hold of a crocodile mistaking it for
a log of wood. If you live for an ideal, let its hold on your
mind be so strong that there is no place for anything else in the
mind. We all know how people spend their energies, time,
bodies, and everything to become rich. It shows that if one
wills, one can direct the same amount of energy and struggle
for freedom. Do you all know how fleeting is wealth for
which we struggle so hard? How much more then should
be the energy you put forth for that which remains with one
for ever. Mind you, this struggle is the great lesson, and if
there is any road to heaven, it is through this hell of a 'struggle'.
When the soul has wrestled with circumstances and has met
death a thousand times on the way, but nothing daunted has
struggled forward again and again and yet again—then the
soul comes out a giant and laughs at the ideal he has been
struggling for; because he finds how much greater is he than
the ideal . . . . Realising my own real nature is the one
goal of my life."

Along with the tremendous determination to struggle, there must be meditation. Meditation is the nearest approach to spiritual life. "It is the one moment in our daily life that we are not at all material, the soul thinking of itself free from all matter—this marvellous touch of the soul." "No breathing, no physical training of Yoga, nothing is of any use until you are poised in the idea 'I am the witness'. How the witness consciousness can change your whole attitude is seen from your experience of seeing a horror scene painted. In real life you are frightened by it, but when you see it painted by an artist, you will enjoy that art. In life you have to feel, "I am in my picture gallery...... I am looking at these successive paintings. They are beautiful, whether good or evil. It is all one, the infinite flames of the great painter......He ......She, the Mother—is playing and we are like dolls, Her helpers in this play. Here She puts one now in the garb of a beggar, another moment in the garb of a king, the next moment in the garb of a saint,and again in the garb of a devil. We are putting on different garbs to help the Mother-Spirit in Her play." There are moments in our life, "when we feel our play is finished; I want to rush to the Mother:......, and then the whole life will seem like a show. We shall see only infinite rythm going on, endless and purposeless, going we do not know where. Only this much shall we say: 'Our play is done!' "

6. The Cosmos and The Self

Everything in Nature arises from fine seed forms, becomes grosser and grosser, exists for a time and again goes back to the original fine form. This is the whole history of Nature and life. Every evolution is, however, preceded by an involution. For example, a tree must be present in the seed, its cause. The whole of the human being is present in that one original protoplasm. Just like that, the whole of this gross universe is present in a seed form as an unmanifest fine cosmic universe, and evolution is its gradual unfoldment. Thus the whole gross universe must have been then in an involved condition before it came out. Its history can be summarised into one unity with two parts—growth and development on the one hand, and decay and death on the other. Where evolution begins, there it must end also. Thus intelligence must be the beginning and the end of the universe. The evolutionists say that intelligence is the last to come in the order of creation. That being so, intelligence must also be the cause of creation. Only in the beginning it is involved. This universal intelligence is what is called God.

A compound is something where causes have combined to become an effect. So these compounded things can come only within the circle of the law of causation. The law holds good only in a universe we experience or imagine. The self of man is beyond the law of causation. He is not therefore a compound or an effect. The Self is therefore ever free and without destruction; nor could it have a beginning or a birth. So the soul is beyond life and death.

The doctrine of monism holds that all that exists forms a unity, a whole, composed of various minute particles. Each one of us is a part, as it were, of that unit. As manifested beings we appear to be separate, but in reality we are one. The more we think ourselves as separate from the whole, the more miserable we become.

7.   Who is a Real Guru?

A real Guru is one who is born from time to time as a repository of a spiritual force which he transmits to future generations through successive links of Gurus and disciples.

This becomes necessary because old religious sects gradually grow lifeless in course of time, and sects with the fire of life become necessary. The truly wise men commit themselves to the particular sect through which the current of life flows.

The one thing necessary for a true disciple is to strip himself of the vanity that he possesses some spiritual wisdom and to surrender himself completely to the guidance of the Guru. The true humility arising out of the feeling that we are quite blind will open the door of our heart to spiritual truths. Truth will never come to us so long as there remains the faintest shadow of Ahankara, arrogant egoism.

8. On Art

The Greek Art aimed at imitating nature to the minutest detail. According to this ideal the painting of a piece of flesh must be realistic enough to attract a dog. The tendency of the Indian art was, on the other hand, to represent the ideal, the supersensual. This became degenerated into painting grotesque images. "Now true art can be compared to a lily which springs on the ground, takes its nourishment from the ground, is in touch with the ground, and yet is high about it." When art loses touch with Nature, it degenerates. While in touch with Nature, it must rise above Nature·

"Art is representing the beautiful, and there must be art in everything. The artistic faculty was highly developed in Sri Ramakrishna."

9. On Language

My ideal of language is my Master's language — most colloquial and yet most expressive.

The best prose in Sanskrit is Patanjali's Mahabhashya. The language of Hitopadesa is not bad.

10. Isvara and Brahman

The Personal God is the same Absolute looked at through the haze of Maya. When we approach Him through the senses, we can see Him only as a Personal God. The idea is that the self cannot be objectified. How can the knower know himself? But it can cast a shadow, as it were, and that can be called objectification. The highest form of objectification of the Self is the Personal God.

Speaking in another context, he said; Isvara is the sum total of all the individuals. Yet He is an Individual as the human body is, with each cell constituting it as an individual unit. The existence of Isvara, therefore, depends on that of the Jiva, as of the self on the body and vice versa. Thus Jiva and Isvara are co-existent beings. When the one exists, the other too must. Because, except on our earth, in all the the higher spheres, the amount of good is vastly in excess of the amount of evil, the sum total (Isvara) may be said to be all-good. Omnipotence and Omniscience are obvious qualities and need no argument to prove apart from the very fact of totality. Brahman is beyond both these and is not a conditioned state. It is the only unit not composed of many units, the Principle which runs through all, from a cell to God, without which nothing can exist. Whatever is real in them, is that Brahman.

11. On Jnana Yoga

Theologians, philosophers and scientists in the West are striving to get a proof that they live after death. This is only a storm in a tea cup, for it is a silly superstition to think that you ever die. No man can imagine his own annihilation. The idea of immortality is inherent in him.

The idea of eternal progress—the theory that we are going on ever and anon in a straight line — is absurd; for, a straight line infinitely projected becomes a circle. So every soul moves in a circle, as it were, and will have to complete the circle and return to the source. No soul goes eternally downward but it has to take an upward curve to complete the circuit. We are all projected from a common centre, which is God, and will go back to Him.

The soul is a circle whose circumference is nowhere (i.e. limitless) and whose centre is in some body. Death is but a change of centre. God is a circle whose circumference is nowhere and whose centre is everywhere. When we get out of the limited centre of a body, we shall realise God as our true self.

All beings are like bits of paper and straw flowing towards the ocean in a tremendous stream. They may struggle to go back or may float against the current and play all sorts of pranks, but in the long run must go and join the great ocean of Life and Bliss.

Jnana (Knowledge) is "creedlessness," but this does not mean that it despises creeds. It only means a stage above all creeds, through which all creeds can be viewed equally.

It is obvious that all knowledge is stored up in us from the beginning. If we are like little waves in the ocean, that ocean is our background.

There is really no difference between matter, mind and spirit. These are only different phases of the experience of the One. This very world seen by the five senses is matter. The wicked see it as hell, the good as heaven, and the perfect as God.

We cannot demonstrate to the senses that Brahman is the only Existence, but we can show that it is the only conclusion we can arrive at ultimately. The multiplicity we see is only like waves on the ocean—a mass of names and forms. The wave forms are temporary and they cannot be shown separately from the substance of the waves. When the form disappears, only the water remains. The mass of water does not depend on the waves but the waves depend on the water as they have no existence apart from it. Such is the case with regard to the multiplicity, the manifestations of Brahman, which have no existence apart from Him. When we perceive the diversity, the unity disappears for us, and as soon as we perceive the unity, the diversity vanishes.

The Spirit is reflected from the mind. It is the light of the Spirit that makes the mind sentient. The minds are like so many mirrors, and love, fear, hatred, virtue etc, are all the reflections of the Spirit in it. When the reflector is base, the reflection is bad.

The Real Existence is without manifestation. We cannot conceive it, because we shall have to conceive through the mind which is itself a manifestation. The glory is that it is inconceivable. The Reality, the Self, is the only thing we know, because in and through It, we know everything else, and yet we cannot perceive It, for how can we know the knower? If we knew It, It would not be the knower but the known. It would be objectified.

12.   What is the Cause of Illusion?

The question is asked—what is the cause of Maya, of the Absolute experiencing multiplicity? The answer can be given only if one can formulate the question logically. Our position is, the Absolute has become this relative existence only apparently. By the very admission of the Absolute being unconditioned, one admits it cannot be acted upon by anything else. In the unconditioned, there cannot be time, space or causation. So your question will amount to: "What caused that which cannot be caused by anything, to be changed into this?" In other words, your question is relevant only regarding the conditioned. But you want to ask this about the unconditioned.

We can therefore only say that ignorance generates the illusion. Here ignorance does not mean something that is not now known but could be known afterwards. It means that in the ordinary sense, what you seek to know cannot be known by the very nature of things, because It is not an object. So it is asked, "by what means can the knower be known?"

13. Evolution

Patanjali's theory of evolution is far better than the modern conception that competition, struggles, wars etc. are the way through which evolution is achieved. Patanjali says, "The change of one species into another is attained by the infilling of Nature." The term 'infilling of Nature' is explained thus: Peasants, irrigate fields by removing the obstructions in the way for the water to flow from the reservoir. So even these struggles and wars are not absolutely necessary for evolution. It is only our impatience that creates them. The struggle we create through our own impatience. The obstacles for growth may be removed by more civilised ways. The highest manifestation of strength is to keep ourselves calm.

14. Buddhism and Vedanta

The Vedanta philosophy is the foundation of Buddhism. But what is called the Advaita philosophy of the modern school has a great many conclusions of the Buddhists. Orthodox Hindu philosophers will not, however. admit this, as they consider Buddhists as heretics.

With the Northern School of Buddhism, we have no quarrel, but we have a difference with the southern Buddhists. The southern Buddhists contend that there is only a phenomenal world and that we Vedantins speak of the noumenal world behind it.   The answer of the Vedantins is that this is a wrong statement of their position.   The Vedantin never says that there is a noumenal and a phenomenal world. There is only One.   Seen through the senses, it is phenomenal; but in reality, it is noumenal all the time.   A man who sees the rope does not see the snake.   It is either the rope or the snake, but never the two.   So the Buddhist statement that we believe in two worlds is entirely false.   The Buddhist can say there is only the phenomenal if he likes, but he has no right to contend that others have no right to say that there is only the noumenal.

15.   Law And Freedom

The sort of freedom which we feel when we are yet in the phenomenal is a glimpse of the real freedom which has not yet been realised.

It is wrong to think that freedom consists in obedience to the laws of Nature.   The history of human progress contradicts this idea; for, it is disobedience of Nature that has resulted in progress.   It may be said that the conquest of lower laws is through the higher.   Even there the conquering mind is only trying to be free.   As soon as it finds that the struggle is through law, it wants to conquer that also.   So the idea of freedom is there, wherever there is growth.   The tree never disobeys law; the cow never steals; and the oyster never tells a lie.   But yet they are not greater than man.   Obedience to law, carried far enough, would make us simply matter, inertia in society or in politics or in religion. Too many laws are a sure sign of death.   Eternal law cannot be called freedom, because to say that the eternal is inside law, is to limit it.

There is no purpose with God because if there were some purpose, He would be nothing better than a man. For He would be bound in that case by something outside Himself. So it is better to say that He simply sports with Nature, and we call this law, because we can see only little bits of it.

In God and freedom we began, and freedom and God will be the end. These laws are in the middle stage through which we have to pass. If there is to be any eternal law binding man all the time, where is the difference between him and a blade of grass?

Man has freedom already but he will have to discover it. The ignorant man is satisfied if he can get freedom within certain limits—if he can get rid of the bondage of hunger or of thirst. But the sage feels that there is a stronger bondage which has to be thrown off. He would not consider the freedom of the Red Indian as freedom at all.

Freedom, not knowledge, is the ultimate goal. Knowledge may be the means to it. The whole history of humanity consists in a series of attempts to go beyond the laws of Nature, impelled by the inherent call of freedom.

By analysis on philosophic grounds, we may find that we are not free, but there will always remain this factor, this consciousness, that I am free. It is this dual experience of ours that has to be explained. The Vedantic solution is that the soul is really free, but that it is its thoughts and actions percolating through the body and mind, that are not free.